my **revisi⏻n** notes

s Centre

ECONOMICS

David Horner

Steve Stoddard

HODDER
EDUCATION
AN HACHETTE UK COMPANY

Hachette UK's policy is to use papers that are natural, renewable and recyclable products and made from wood grown in sustainable forests. The logging and manufacturing processes are expected to conform to the environmental regulations of the country of origin.

Orders: please contact Bookpoint Ltd, 130 Park Drive, Milton Park, Abingdon, Oxon OX14 4SB. Telephone: (44) 01235 827720. Fax: (44) 01235 400454. Email education@ bookpoint.co.uk

Lines are open from 9 a.m. to 5 p.m., Monday to Saturday, with a 24-hour message answering service. You can also order through our website: www.hoddereducation.co.uk

ISBN: 978 1 4718 6584 8

© David Horner and Steve Stoddard 2016

First published in 2016 by

Hodder Education,
An Hachette UK Company
Carmelite House
50 Victoria Embankment
London EC4Y 0DZ
www.hoddereducation.co.uk

Impression number   10 9 8 7 6 5 4 3 2 1
Year   2020 2019 2018 2017 2016

Cover photo reproduced by permission of Alena Yakusheva/Fotolia

Typeset by Integra Software Services Pvt. Ltd, Pondicherry, India

Printed in Spain

A catalogue record for this title is available from the British Library.

Get the most from this book

Everyone has to decide his or her own revision strategy, but it is essential to review your work, learn it and test your understanding. These Revision Notes will help you to do that in a planned way, topic by topic. Use this book as the cornerstone of your revision and don't hesitate to write in it — personalise your notes and check your progress by ticking off each section as you revise.

Tick to track your progress

Use the revision planner on pages 4 and 5 to plan your revision, topic by topic. Tick each box when you have:

● revised and understood a topic
● tested yourself
● practised the exam questions and gone online to check your answers and complete the quick quizzes

You can also keep track of your revision by ticking off each topic heading in the book. You may find it helpful to add your own notes as you work through each topic.

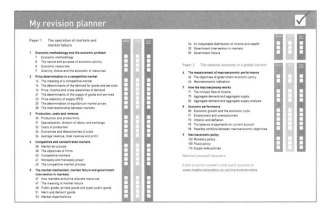

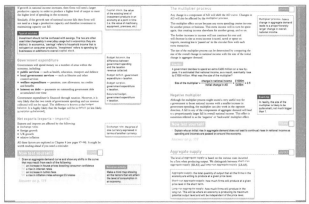

Features to help you succeed

Examiners' tips and summaries

Expert tips are given throughout the book to help you polish your exam technique in order to maximise your chances in the exam. The summaries provide a quick-check bullet list for each topic.

Typical mistakes

The authors identify the typical mistakes candidates make and explain how you can avoid them.

Now test yourself

These short, knowledge-based questions provide the first step in testing your learning. Answers are at the back of the book.

Definitions and key words

Clear, concise definitions of essential key terms are provided where they first appear.

Key words from the specification are highlighted in bold throughout the book.

Revision activities

These activities will help you to understand each topic in an interactive way.

Debates

Debates are highlighted to help you assess arguments and use evidence appropriately.

Exam practice

Practice exam questions are provided for each topic. Use them to consolidate your revision and practise your exam skills.

Online

Go online to check your answers to the exam questions and try out the extra quick quizzes at **www.hoddereducation.co.uk/myrevisionnotes**

My revision planner

	REVISED	TESTED	EXAM READY

Exam practice answers and quick quizzes at
www.hoddereducation.co.uk/myrevisionnotes

Countdown to my exams

6–8 weeks to go

- Start by looking at the specification — make sure you know exactly what material you need to revise and the style of the examination. Use the revision planner on pages 4 and 5 to familiarise yourself with the topics.
- Organise your notes, making sure you have covered everything on the specification. The revision planner will help you to group your notes into topics.
- Work out a realistic revision plan that will also allow you time for relaxation. Set aside days and times for all the subjects you need to study, and stick to your timetable.
- Set yourself sensible targets. Break your revision down into focused sessions of around 40 minutes, divided by breaks. These *Revision Notes* organise the basic facts into short, memorable sections to make revising easier.

REVISED ☐

2–5 weeks to go

- Read through the relevant sections of this book and refer to the exam tips, summaries, typical mistakes and key terms. Tick off the topics as you feel confident about them. Highlight those you find difficult and look at them again in detail.
- Test your understanding of each topic by working through the 'Now test yourself' questions in the book. Look up the answers at the back of the book.
- Make a note of any problem areas as you revise, and ask your teacher to go over these in class.
- Look at past papers. They are one of the best ways to revise and to practise your exam skills. Write or prepare planned answers to the 'Exam practice' questions in this book. Check your answers online and try out the extra quick quizzes at www.hoddereducation.co.uk/myrevisionnotes
- Use the revision activities to try out different revision methods. For example, you can make notes using mind maps, spider diagrams or flash cards.
- Track your progress using the revision planner and give yourself a reward when you have achieved your target!

REVISED ☐

One week to go

- Try to fit in at least one more timed practice of an entire past paper and seek feedback from your teacher, comparing your work closely with the mark scheme.
- Check the revision planner to make sure you haven't missed any topics. Brush up on any areas of difficulty by talking them over with a friend or getting help from your teacher.
- Attend any revision classes put on by your teacher. Remember, he or she is an expert at preparing people for examinations.

REVISED ☐

The day before the examination

- Flick through these *Revision Notes* for useful reminders — for example, the exam tips, summaries, typical mistakes and key terms.
- Check the time and place of your examination.
- Make sure you have everything you need — extra pens and pencils, tissues, a watch, bottled water, sweets.
- Allow some time to relax and have an early night to ensure you are fresh and alert for the examinations.

REVISED ☐

My exams

AS Economics Paper 1

Date:..

Time:..

Location:..

AS Economics Paper 2

Date:..

Time:..

Location:..

Economic methodology

Economics is the study of how the world's scarce resources are allocated to competing uses to satisfy society's wants.

As a social science, Economics attempts to adopt a scientific methodology for observing the behaviour of individuals and groups and then makes predictions based upon these observations. For example, how many more units of a product might an individual buy if the price of that product is reduced by 25%?

Positive economic statements

REVISED

Positive economic statements are objective statements that can be tested against facts to be declared either true or false. A positive economic statement does not necessarily have to be true.

> **Positive statement**: an objective statement that can be tested against the facts to be declared either true or false.

Normative economic statements

REVISED

Normative economic statements are subjective opinions or value judgements that cannot be tested against facts. These often concern views about what individuals, firms or governments *should* do, based upon people's ethical, moral or political standpoint. Some economists view such statements as being the concern of the field of politics rather than economics. However, much of economic policy rests on normative judgements about the 'right' levels of, for example, taxes, minimum wages or the amount of government intervention in markets.

> **Normative statement**: a subjective opinion, or value judgement, that cannot be declared either true or false.

> **Typical mistake**
>
> A positive statement need not necessarily be factually true. It simply needs to be capable of being tested to be declared true or false.

Now test yourself

TESTED

1 Which of the following would be classed as a normative economic statement?
   A An increase in price usually leads to a fall in the quantity demanded of a good.
   B The government should spend more money on improving public transport.
   C A reduction in income tax will lead to more people choosing to work.
   D An increase in price usually leads to a rise in the quantity supplied of a good.

Answer on p. 117

The nature and purpose of economic activity

Needs, wants and economic welfare

The main purpose of economic activity is to satisfy society's needs and wants.

A **need** is something that humans require to survive, such as food, shelter and warmth. A **want** is something not essential for survival, but which people feel improves their standard of living, or **economic welfare**, e.g. a new car.

Economic welfare refers to the standard of living, or general wellbeing, of individuals in society. Satisfying society's needs and wants in terms of material and non-material things leads, in general, to increased economic welfare. Increasing real gross domestic product (GDP) per capita is pursued in order for average living standards to increase, as this allows people to be able to satisfy more of their needs and wants. There is debate, however, about whether people feel genuinely happier simply by having more of their wants satisfied.

> **Need**: something which humans need to survive, e.g. food, shelter and warmth.
>
> **Want**: something which people feel improves their standard of living but is not required for survival.
>
> **Economic welfare**: the standard of living or general wellbeing of people in society.

Economic resources

A country's economic resources are known as the **factors of production**. Four are usually identified:

- **Capital:** man-made physical equipment used to make other goods and services. This includes machinery and computer equipment.
- **Enterprise:** entrepreneurs are individuals who take a business risk in combining the other three factors of production in order to produce a good or service.
- **Land:** all naturally occurring resources such as minerals, the sea, fertile land and the environment. These can be further divided into renewable and non-renewable resources.
- **Labour:** people involved in production, sometimes referred to as human capital.

> **Factors of production**: a country's productive economic resources, divided into capital, enterprise, land and labour.

> **Typical mistake**
>
> Don't confuse the term 'capital' for 'money' in economics. Money is classed as financial capital.

Now test yourself

2 Which of the following would be classified as land by an economist?
    A   a sewing machine
    B   a taxi driver
    C   oil in the North Sea
    D   a laptop computer

Answer on p. 117

> **Exam tip**
>
> The four factors of production can be memorised using the acronym CELL, standing for capital, enterprise, land and labour.

Scarcity, choice and the allocation of resources

The basic economic problem

REVISED

The **basic economic problem** is that of scarcity, i.e. that economic resources are limited relative to society's wants. This means that choices must be made when deciding how to allocate these resources. In so doing, the three fundamental economic questions must be considered:

1 **What to produce and in what quantities?** Goods are usually divided into consumer goods and capital goods. Consumer goods are those that give satisfaction to consumers, such as pizza or a fridge freezer. Capital goods are those used to produce other goods, including machinery and IT equipment.

2 **How should goods and services be produced?** The basic production decision is between labour-intensive methods (where a high proportion of human capital is used compared to capital) or capital-intensive methods (the opposite).

3 **To whom should goods and services be allocated?** This choice affects the degrees of equity and equality in society. Decisions about who in society gets what will be determined by the economic system that prevails. Two extreme forms of economic system are:

- **The free market or capitalist economy.** Decisions are made solely by the interactions of consumers and firms, with no government intervention.

- **The command or centrally planned economy.** Decisions are made solely by the planning department of governments.

> **Basic economic problem**: scarce economic resources compared with society's unlimited wants.

Now test yourself

TESTED

3 Why do individuals, firms and governments have to make choices about what to produce?
4 How might decisions about the three fundamental economic questions differ between a free market economy and a centrally planned economy?

Answer on p. 117

Opportunity cost

REVISED

In making any choice regarding how to allocate scarce resources, something must be given up. This is the concept of **opportunity cost**, i.e. that scarce resources have competing uses. It means that when someone chooses one use, they must forgo the next best alternative use.

> **Opportunity cost**: the cost of the next best alternative that you give up when you have to make a choice.

Now test yourself

TESTED

5 John bought a German saloon car for £10 000 2 years ago. A new car would cost £13 000. He could sell his German saloon car for £8000. What is the present opportunity cost of keeping his car?

  A £10 000   C £3000

  B £13 000   D £8000

Answer on p. 117

Economic goods and free goods

Economic goods are those that use up scarce economic resources in their production. These include most consumer goods.

Free goods are unlimited in their supply and availability, such as sunlight or air, and thus the opportunity cost of consuming them is zero.

> **Economic good**: a good that has an opportunity cost in consumption because it uses up scarce resources.
>
> **Free good**: a good that does not have an opportunity cost in consumption because it does not use up scarce resources.

Production possibility diagrams

A **production possibility curve (PPC)** is a diagram which depicts the maximum combinations of two goods that can be produced by an economy, assuming all resources are fully employed and used efficiently. Figure 1.1 shows a PPC.

> **Production possibility curve (PPC)**: a diagram which shows the maximum possible output combinations of two goods in an economy, assuming full employment of efficient resources.

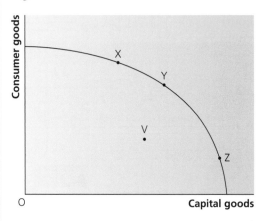

Figure 1.1 A production possibility curve (PPC)

Any point on the production possibility curve, e.g. X, Y or Z, implies that all factors of production are fully employed. An economy operating at point V must therefore be operating inefficiently, with unused resources, e.g. unemployed labour or idle machines.

> **Exam tip**
>
> Production possibility diagrams may also be referred to as production possibility frontiers (PPFs) and production possibility boundaries (PPBs).

Shifts of the PPC

Factors leading to shifts of the PPC, outwards or inwards, are driven by changes in the quantity and efficiency (quality) of the factors of production.

Factors causing an outward shift of the PPC

- Technological improvements that lead to increased productivity of capital equipment.
- Discovery of new resources, e.g. oil and gas.
- Improvements in education and training that lead to a more productive workforce.
- Changes that lead to an increase in working population, e.g. increases in immigration or a raised retirement age.

Factors causing an inward shift of the PPC

- Disasters such as earthquakes or floods that devastate productive resources.

> **Typical mistake**
>
> Do not confuse an increased utilisation of factors of production with economic growth. An increased utilisation of factors of production moves the economy to a point closer to the PPC, whereas economic growth leads to an outward shift of the PPC.

- Wars.
- Global warming/climate change, which may lead to loss of farmland, rising sea levels and more extreme weather.
- A prolonged recession, which may lead to permanent loss of productive capacity if businesses close down and/or workers lose skills.

Using a PPC diagram to show opportunity cost

The PPC in Figure 1.2 shows the maximum combinations of consumer goods and capital goods that can be produced with a given set of factors of production.

The diagram shows the concept of opportunity cost — as more capital goods are produced, more consumer goods must be given up. An increase in the amount of capital goods from 0M to 0S leads to a loss of output of consumer goods from 0L to 0R.

A subsequent increase in production of capital goods from 0S to 0V leads to a proportionately larger fall in production of consumer goods from 0R to 0T.

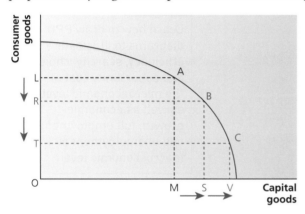

Figure 1.2 The production possibility curve and opportunity cost

Using a PPC diagram to show economic growth

Production possibility diagrams can also be used to show **economic growth**.

The PPC in Figure 1.3 again shows the maximum combinations of consumer goods and capital goods that can be produced with a given set of factors of production. We will assume that the economy is producing at point A on the current PPC.

> **Economic growth**: an increase in the productive capacity of an economy over time.

An improvement in technology, or any of the factors that lead to an outward shift of the PPC, mean that there has been an increase in the productive capacity of the economy. This will lead to the entire PPC shifting outwards. Production at point E is now possible, leading to increased potential output of both capital goods and consumer goods.

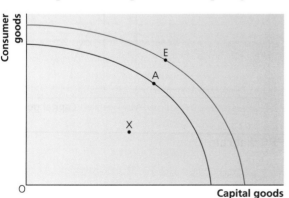

Figure 1.3 The production possibility curve and economic growth

> **Typical mistake**
>
> A movement from point X to point A is not economic growth — it is simply an economy making fuller use of its existing, previously unemployed, resources.

Economic efficiency and production possibility diagrams

The two main types of economic efficiency are **productive efficiency** and **allocative efficiency**. Productive efficiency is concerned with how well society uses its scarce resources to maximise outputs of goods and services.

At the level of a whole economy, productive efficiency occurs when maximum output is produced from the available factors of production, which would be at any point on the PPC. By definition then, any point that lies inside the PPC is productively inefficient.

The concepts of productive efficiency and productive inefficiency are shown in the PPC diagram in Figure 1.4.

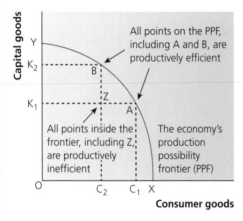

Productive efficiency: when maximum output is produced from the available factors of production and when it is not possible to produce more of one good or service without producing less of another.

Allocative efficiency: when an economy's factors of production are used to produce the combination of goods and services that maximises society's welfare.

Figure 1.4 Productive efficiency and the PPC

Allocative efficiency exists when an economy's factors of production are used to produce the combination of goods and services that maximises society's welfare. The PPC shows all possible efficient combinations of goods and services that can be produced, but does not specify an allocatively efficient point. The allocatively efficient point on the PPC is the one that best reflects society's preferences for particular goods and services.

Now test yourself

TESTED

6 With reference to the figure:
   (a) What is the significance of point Z?
   (b) Explain why points A and B can be considered productively efficient.
   (c) How might point Y be achieved in the future?
   (d) Explain how the diagram can be used to show the concept of opportunity cost.

7 Explain the effect on a PPC of the following:
   (a) improvements in soil fertility resulting from the use of chemicals
   (b) a decrease in population size due to falling birth rates
   (c) technological improvements in capital equipment
   (d) increased government spending on education and training

Answers on p. 117

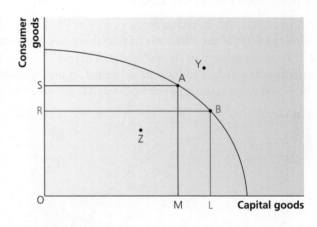

A PPC diagram

Exam practice

1 Which statement is true?
  A A positive economic statement never contains words such as 'should' or 'ought to'.
  B A positive economic statement is one that can be tested against the facts.
  C A normative statement never contains words such as 'will' or 'does'.
  D A normative statement can be scientifically proven.   [1]
2 Scarcity in an economy means that:
  A There is a misallocation of resources.
  B There are no free goods.
  C People must make choices.
  D It is not possible to maximise economic welfare.   [1]
3 When money is used as a medium of exchange:
  A Trade is likely to increase.
  B Specialisation and the division of labour are impossible.
  C Barter becomes more widespread.
  D Prices must increase.   [1]
4 Which of the following is a factor of production?
  A a loan from a bank
  B profits made by businesses
  C labour productivity
  D a computer   [1]
5 The diagram shows an economy's production possibility curve.
  Which of the following combinations of consumer goods and
  capital goods is achievable with current factors of production?
  A only A
  B only B and C
  C A, B, C and D
  D only A, B and C   [1]

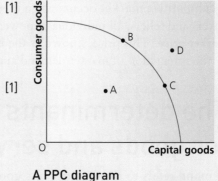

A PPC diagram

ONLINE

Summary

You should have an understanding of:
● The meaning of the term 'economics'.
● Basic economic methodology.
● The nature and purpose of economic activity.
● The difference between needs and wants.
● Positive and normative economic statements.
● The meaning of scarcity and how this leads to choices having to be made.
● The four key factors of production: capital, enterprise, land and labour.
● The difference between consumer goods and capital goods.

● The concept of opportunity cost and its significance for individuals, firms and governments.
● The difference between economic goods and free goods.
● Production possibility curves and how to draw them correctly.
● How to use PPCs to illustrate opportunity cost, efficiency and economic growth.

Answers and quick quizzes online

The meaning of a competitive market

A **market** is a situation in which buyers and sellers come together to engage in trade. In the modern age, a market does not have to occur in a physical location, with e-commerce now playing an increasingly important role in the exchange of goods and services.

A **competitive market** occurs when there are a large number of potential buyers and sellers, all individually powerless to influence the ruling market price. This price, known as the **equilibrium price**, is determined by the interaction of market demand and market supply.

> **Market**: a situation in which buyers and sellers come together to engage in trade.
>
> **Competitive market**: a situation where there is a large number of potential buyers and sellers with abundant information about the market.
>
> **Equilibrium price**: the price at which the planned demand of consumers equals the planned supply of firms.

The determinants of the demand for goods and services

Demand refers to the quantity of a good or service that consumers are willing and able to buy at given prices in a particular time period. Economists are concerned with **effective demand**, i.e. desire for a product backed up by the ability to pay, rather than an unfulfilled want.

> **Demand**: the quantity of a good or service that consumers are willing and able to buy at given prices in a particular time period.
>
> **Effective demand**: consumers' desire to buy a good, backed up by the ability to pay.

The law of demand and the shape of the market demand curve

REVISED

The law of demand states that as the price of a good or service falls, the quantity demanded increases. This inverse relationship between the price and quantity demanded of a good or service is shown in Figure 2.1. In analysing the effect of a change in price on quantity demanded, we usually assume that all other possible determinants of demand are held constant. Economists refer to this assumption as 'ceteris paribus'. An increase in the quantity demanded resulting from a fall in price is known as an extension of demand, whereas a fall in quantity demanded resulting from an increase in price is known as a contraction of demand.

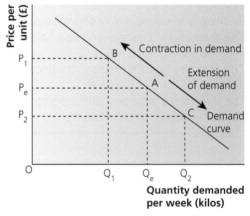

Figure 2.1 Movements along a demand curve

Using graph paper, construct a demand curve to show the information shown in the table.

Price of coffee (£ per kilo)	Quantity of coffee demanded per week (kilos)
18	150 000
15	200 000
12	250 000
9	300 000
6	350 000
3	400 000

Shifts of a demand curve

REVISED

A mistake that students often make is in confusing a movement along a demand curve with a shift of the whole demand curve. As previously explained, the only variable that leads to a movement along a given demand curve is a change in price of that good or service. Factors that may lead to a shift in the position of the demand curve are referred to as the **conditions of demand**.

These include:
- **Real disposable incomes:** the incomes of individuals after the effects of inflation, **taxation** and benefits are taken into account.
- **Tastes and preferences (fashions):** the popularity of goods and services is often influenced by changes in society's preferences and may be influenced by the media, advertising and technological change.
- **Population:** the size, age and gender composition of the population will affect the market size for many products.
- **Prices of substitute products:** **substitute** products are those in competitive demand that may be seen as close alternatives to a particular good or service.
- **Prices of complementary products:** **complementary** products are those in joint demand, i.e. demanded together with other goods or services.

Conditions of demand: factors other than the price of the good that lead to a change in position of the demand curve.

Taxation: a charge placed by the government on various forms of economic activity. Most taxes are on forms of income and types of spending.

Substitute: a good that may be consumed as an alternative to another good.

Complement: a good that tends to be consumed together with another good.

If any of these factors changes, then the demand curve for the good or service in question will change. This leads to either a rightward or a leftward shift of the demand curve, as shown in Figure 2.2. A rightward shift is known as an increase in demand, whereas a leftward shift is known as a decrease in demand. A rightward shift means that a greater quantity of a good or service is demanded at any given price, whereas a leftward shift means that a lower quantity of a good or service is demanded at any given price.

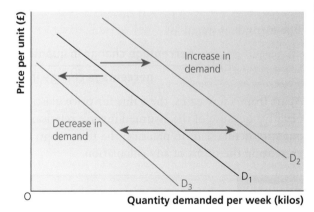

Figure 2.2 Shifts of the demand curve

Now test yourself

TESTED

1 What would be the effect of the following on demand for cars in the UK?
   (a) an increase in petrol prices
   (b) a decrease in car parking fees
   (c) a fall in rail fares
   (d) an increase in fuel efficiency of cars

Answer on p. 117

Price, income and cross elasticities of demand

Price elasticity of demand (PED)

REVISED

Price elasticity of demand refers to the responsiveness of the quantity demanded of a good or service to a change in its price.

The formula is stated as:

$$PED = \frac{\text{percentage change in quantity demanded}}{\text{percentage change in price}}$$

Apart from a few cases, the value for price elasticity of demand is negative because of the assumed inverse relationship between price and quantity demanded. In practice, the minus sign tends to be ignored when presenting the result of any calculation.

> **Price elasticity of demand**: the responsiveness of quantity demanded of a good to a change in price.

Exam tip

It is worth memorising the percentage change formula as you will be required to use it frequently.

$$\text{Percentage change} = \left(\frac{\text{change}}{\text{original value}}\right) \times 100$$

Key values and diagrams

Price inelastic demand

When demand for a product is price inelastic, the value of PED is between 0 and 1, ignoring the minus sign.

Example — a 50% increase in the price of petrol leads to a 10% fall in quantity demanded. So:

$$PED = \frac{-10}{+50} = -0.2$$

The change in price has led to a smaller percentage change in the quantity demanded.

Price elastic demand

When demand for a product is price elastic, the value of PED is greater than 1, ignoring the minus sign.

Example — a 10% reduction in the price of cars leads to a 15% increase in quantity demanded. So:

$$PED = \frac{+15}{-10} = -1.5$$

The change in price has led to a larger percentage change in the quantity demanded.

Figures 2.3(a) and 2.3(b) illustrate an inelastic and inelastic section of a demand curve.

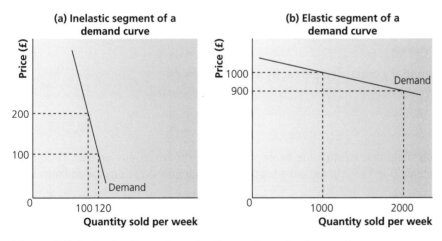

Figure 2.3 An inelastic and an elastic section of a demand curve

Unitary elastic demand

When demand is unitary elastic, the value of PED is exactly 1, ignoring the minus sign. The demand curve is a rectangular hyperbola, as shown in Figure 2.4.

Example — a 20% increase in the price of a mobile phone leads to a 20% decrease in quantity demanded. So:

$$PED = \frac{-20}{+20} = -1.0$$

The change in price has led to the same percentage change in quantity demanded.

Perfectly inelastic demand

When demand for a product is perfectly price inelastic, the value of PED is 0. The demand curve will be vertical, as shown in Figure 2.4.

Example — a 10% increase in the price of a carton of milk leads to no change in quantity demanded. So:

$$PED = \frac{0}{+10} = 0.0$$

The change in price has led to no change in quantity demanded.

Perfectly elastic demand

When demand is perfectly elastic, the value of PED is infinity. The demand curve will be horizontal as shown in Figure 2.4.

Example — an extremely small increase in the price of a product leads to the quantity demanded falling to zero.

The change in price has led to an infinitely large change in quantity demanded.

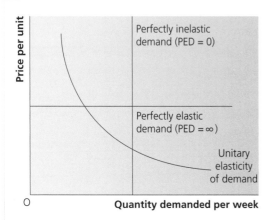

Figure 2.4 Demand curves showing unitary elasticity, perfectly inelastic and perfectly elastic demand

TESTED

2 Calculate the price elasticity of demand in the following examples and comment briefly on your results:
  (a) A rise in the price of petrol from 100p to 120p per litre leads to a fall in quantity demanded from 50 to 45 litres per week.
  (b) A fall in the price of games consoles from £250 to £200 leads to a rise in quantity demanded from 100 to 150 per day.
  (c) A rise in the price of racing bicycles from £2400 to £2640 leads to a reduction in quantity demanded from 60 to 40 per month.

Answer on p. 117

Price elasticity of demand and total revenue

The price elasticity of demand of a product determines what happens to consumer spending (and therefore total revenue) following a price change.
- If demand is price elastic, a reduction in price leads to an increase in total revenue.
- If demand is price inelastic, a reduction in price leads to a decrease in total revenue.
- If demand is price elastic, a price increase leads to a reduction in total revenue.
- If demand is price inelastic, a price increase leads to an increase in total revenue.

3 The initial price of tea bags is £1.50 per box and quantity demanded is 3000 boxes per week. Following a sales promotion, price is reduced to £1.20 per box and quantity demanded becomes 3300 per week as a result. Calculate both the change in total revenue and the price elasticity of demand.

4 If demand for holidays to the Maldives is price elastic, what will happen to total revenue if holiday companies increase their prices for holidays to this destination?

5 If an increase in the price of milk leads to a rise in total revenue, what can be concluded about price elasticity of demand?

Answer on p. 117

Determinants of price elasticity of demand

The following factors will influence the price elasticity of demand for a good or service:

- **Availability of close substitutes:** if a very close substitute exists for a product, an increase in its price will lead to consumers buying more of the substitute. If one or more close substitutes exist, this will tend to make demand for the product price elastic. If there are few close substitutes, demand will be more inelastic.
- **Percentage of income spent on the product:** if a product accounts for a relatively large percentage of a consumer's income, such as a new car, a change in price of, say, 50% is likely to have a significant impact upon disposable income. Therefore demand for such products will tend to be price elastic. However, the same proportional price change for a relatively inexpensive product such as a loaf of bread will not have the same overall impact upon disposable income and so consumers are likely to be less sensitive to changes in price. Therefore demand for such products will tend to be price inelastic.
- **Nature of the product:** if a product is seen as a necessity, or perhaps even has addictive qualities, demand will tend to be price inelastic, as few alternatives will exist from the viewpoint of the consumer. However, if a product is seen as a luxury, i.e. something that a consumer can do without, demand will tend to be price elastic.
- **Time period:** the longer the time period following a price change, the easier it is for a consumer to adjust their spending patterns, to research alternatives, and for more alternatives to become available. In the very short run, motorists may feel obliged to pay whatever price they are charged per litre of fuel, and so demand will be more price inelastic. In the long run, motorists may be able to switch to alternative fuels, more fuel-efficient cars, use public transport or move closer to work. This will make demand for a product more price elastic in the long run.
- **Broad or specific market definition:** a broad market category, e.g. food, is likely to have price inelastic demand, whereas a specific product in a market segment, e.g. baked beans produced by a particular firm, is likely to have more price elastic demand.

Income elasticity of demand (YED)   REVISED ☐

Income elasticity of demand measures the responsiveness of demand to a change in real income. The formula is:

$$YED = \frac{\text{percentage change in quantity demanded}}{\text{percentage change in real income}}$$

> **Income elasticity of demand:** the responsiveness of demand for a good to a change in consumers' real income.

Key values

For YED the sign is important. If the value is positive, i.e. greater than 0, the product is a normal good. This means a rise in income will lead to an increase in demand. If the value is negative, i.e. less than 0, the product is an inferior good. This means a rise in income will lead to a fall in demand.

Income elastic demand

When demand for a product is income elastic, the value of YED is greater than +1.

Example — a 10% increase in real income leads to a 20% increase in demand for foreign holidays. So:

$$YED = \frac{+20}{+10} = +2.0$$

The increase in real income has led to a greater percentage increase in demand. Income elastic products are often referred to as luxury goods.

Income inelastic demand

When demand for a product is income inelastic, the value of YED is between 0 and +1.

Example — a 10% increase in real income leads to a 2% increase in demand for cartons of milk. So:

$$YED = \frac{+2}{+10} = +0.2$$

The increase in real income has led to a smaller percentage increase in demand. Income inelastic products are often referred to as basic goods or necessities.

Negative income elasticity

When demand for a product is negative income elastic, the value of YED is negative, i.e. less than 0.

Example — a 20% increase in real income leads to a 10% fall in demand for a supermarket's value brand of baked beans. So:

$$YED = \frac{-10}{+20} = -0.5$$

The increase in income has led to a fall in demand. Negative income elastic products are referred to as inferior goods.

Now test yourself

TESTED

6 In each of the following cases, calculate the income elasticity of demand and comment upon your answer:
   (a) A 7% increase in real incomes causes a 21% fall in demand for a supermarket's own brand of chocolate biscuits.
   (b) A 10% increase in real incomes causes a 25% increase in demand for holidays to Barbados.
   (c) An 8% fall in real incomes leads to a 32% fall in demand for fillet steak.

Answer on p. 117

Cross elasticity of demand (XED)

Cross elasticity of demand measures the responsiveness of the demand for a product following a change in price of another product.

The formula is:

$$XED = \frac{\text{percentage change in quantity demanded of product A}}{\text{percentage change in price of product B}}$$

> **Cross elasticity of demand**: the responsiveness of the demand for a product following a change in price of another product.

Key values

For XED the sign is again important.

A positive value indicates that products A and B are substitutes, i.e. a rise in the price of product B leads to an increase in demand for product A.

A negative value indicates that products A and B are complements, i.e. a rise in price of product B leads to a fall in the demand for product A.

Example — a 20% increase in the price of cod leads to a 10% fall in the demand for chips. So:

$$XED = \frac{-10}{+20} = -0.5$$

The two products are therefore complements.

Now test yourself

7 In each of the following cases calculate the cross elasticity of demand and comment upon your answer:
   (a) A 20% rise in the price of butter leads to a 15% rise in the demand for margarine.
   (b) A 10% rise in the price of strawberries leads to an 8% fall in the demand for fresh cream.

Answer on p. 117

The determinants of the supply of goods and services

> **Supply**: The quantity of a good or service that firms plan to sell at given prices in a particular time period.

Supply refers to the quantity of a good or service that firms plan to sell at given prices in a particular time period.

The law of supply

The law of supply states that as price increases the quantity supplied will increase. This positive relationship is shown in Figure 2.5. Firms are assumed to want to maximise their profits and so a higher price gives an incentive for firms to increase production.

As with demand, a change in price will lead to a movement along an existing supply curve. An increase in price will lead to an increase in quantity supplied, known as an extension in supply. Conversely, a decrease in price will lead to a decrease in quantity supplied, known as a contraction in supply.

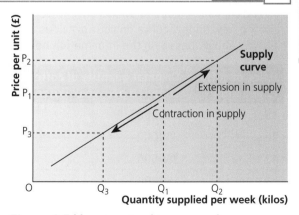

Figure 2.5 Movements along a supply curve

Using graph paper, construct a supply curve to show the information in the table.

Price of coffee (£ per kilo)	Quantity of coffee supplied per week (kilos)
18	400 000
15	350 000
12	300 000
9	250 000
6	200 000
3	150 000

Shifts of a supply curve

Several non-price factors may lead to a shift of the supply curve. These are known as the **conditions of supply**:

- **Production costs:** these include wage costs, raw material costs, energy costs, building rent and interest on borrowing.
- **Productivity of labour:** this refers to the output per worker per hour. This can be affected by the amount of training offered and the quality of capital equipment used by workers.
- **Taxes on businesses:** these include excise duties, VAT and business rates.
- **Production subsidies:** these are government grants to firms to encourage greater production.
- **Technology:** improvements in technology may lead to increased productivity of firms.

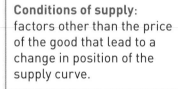

Conditions of supply: factors other than the price of the good that lead to a change in position of the supply curve.

If any of these factors changes, then the supply curve for the good or service in question will change. This leads either to a rightward or leftward shift of the supply curve as shown in Figure 2.6. A rightward shift is known as an increase in supply, whereas a leftward shift is known as a decrease in supply. A rightward shift means that a greater quantity of a good or service is supplied at any given price, whereas a leftward shift means that a lower quantity of a good or service is supplied at any given price.

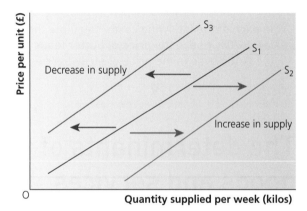

Figure 2.6 Shifts of a supply curve

Assume that warm weather leads to a better coffee harvest than expected, which leads to an increase in supply at every given price. Draw a new supply curve on your previous graph (see the Revision activity above) based on the information below.

Price of coffee (£ per kilo)	Original quantity of coffee supplied per week (kilos)	New quantity of coffee supplied per week (kilos)
18	400 000	430 000
15	350 000	380 000
12	300 000	330 000
9	250 000	280 000
6	200 000	230 000
3	150 000	180 000

Price elasticity of supply (PES)

Price elasticity of supply measures the responsiveness of the quantity supplied of a good or service to a change in price.

The formula is:

$$PES = \frac{\text{percentage change in quantity supplied}}{\text{percentage change in price}}$$

Key values and diagrams

REVISED

Price elasticity of supply will always have a positive value because of the direct relationship between price and quantity supplied.

Price inelastic supply

When the supply of a product is price inelastic, the value of PES is between 0 and 1.

Example — a 20% increase in the price of barley leads to a 5% increase in quantity supplied. So:

$$PES = \frac{+5}{+20} = +0.25$$

The change in price has led to a smaller percentage change in quantity supplied. The supply curve will be relatively steep, as shown in Figure 2.7.

Price elastic supply

When the supply of a product is price elastic, the value of PES is greater than 1.

Example — a 5% fall in the price of carpets leads to a 10% fall in quantity supplied. So:

$$PES = \frac{-10}{-5} = -2.0$$

The change in price has led to a greater percentage increase in quantity supplied. The supply curve will be relatively shallow, as shown in Figure 2.7.

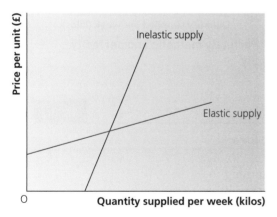

Figure 2.7 Inelastic and elastic supply

Unitary elastic supply

When the supply of a product is unitary elastic, the value of PES is exactly 1. The supply curve is any straight line drawn through the origin, as shown in Figure 2.8.

Example — a 15% increase in the price of table salt leads to a 15% increase in quantity supplied. So:

$$PE = \frac{+15}{+15} = +1.0$$

The change in price has led to the same percentage change in quantity supplied.

Perfectly inelastic supply

When the supply of a product is perfectly inelastic, the value of PES is zero.

Example — a 5% increase in the price of copper leads to zero increase in the quantity supplied. So:

$$PES = \frac{0}{+5} = 0$$

The change in price has led to zero change in the quantity supplied. The supply curve is vertical as in Figure 2.9.

Perfectly elastic supply

When the supply of a product is perfectly elastic, the value of PES is infinity.

Example — a 2% increase in the price of a downloadable song leads to an infinitely large increase in quantity supplied.

The supply curve for perfectly elastic supply is horizontal as in Figure 2.9.

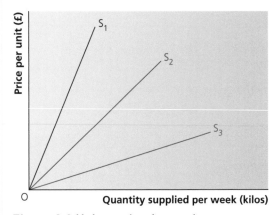

Figure 2.8 Unitary elastic supply

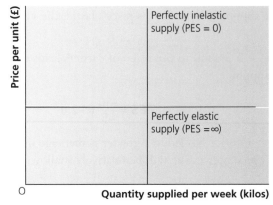

Figure 2.9 Perfectly inelastic and perfectly elastic supply

Determinants of price elasticity of supply REVISED

The following factors will influence the price elasticity of supply for a good or service:

- **Time taken to expand supply:** if it is difficult or time consuming to increase production, e.g. building a new oil refinery, then supply will tend to be more price inelastic.
- **Size of spare capacity:** firms with machinery, factory space or labour that is not fully utilised will be more able to expand production in the short run. Supply will therefore tend to be more price elastic.
- **Available stocks:** firms with stocks of finished or partly finished goods will be able to respond relatively quickly to a price increase and so supply will tend to be more price elastic.

- **Ease of switching production:** if firms can easily adjust the way they use their factors of production, such as capital and labour, to respond to changes in prices, then supply will tend to be relatively price elastic. However, if a firm has highly specialised equipment and employees, supply will tend to be relatively price inelastic.

The determination of equilibrium market prices

The equilibrium market price and quantity are determined by the interaction of the market demand and supply curve for a particular good or service, as shown in Figure 2.10.

When the quantity demanded equals the quantity supplied in a market for a particular product, the market is in a state of equilibrium. The market will continue to be in a state of equilibrium until one of the conditions of demand or supply changes.

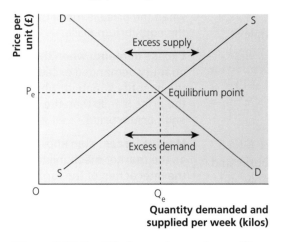

Figure 2.10 Equilibrium price and quantity

Revision activity			
Construct a demand curve and a supply curve on graph paper based on the information in the table. Find the equilibrium price and quantity on your diagram.	**Price of coffee (£ per kilo)**	**Quantity of coffee demanded per week (kilos)**	**Quantity of coffee supplied per week (kilos)**
	18	150 000	400 000
	15	200 000	350 000
	12	250 000	300 000
	9	300 000	250 000
	6	350 000	200 000
	3	400 000	150 000

Market disequilibrium

REVISED

Market disequilibrium occurs when the quantity demanded does not equal the quantity supplied. This is illustrated in Figure 2.11.

> **Market disequilibrium**: a situation where the quantity demanded does not equal the quantity supplied.

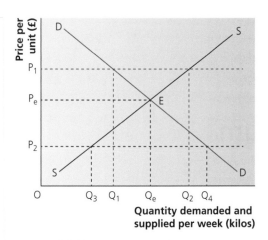

Figure 2.11 Excess demand and excess supply

If the price is above the market equilibrium price of P_e, for example at P_1, then there will be **excess supply**. As shown in the diagram, the quantity demanded is only at Q_1, whilst the relatively high price encourages a greater quantity to be supplied at Q_2. The amount of excess supply is thus $Q_2 - Q_1$.

If the price is below the market equilibrium price of P_e, for example at P_2, then there will be **excess demand**. As shown in the diagram, the quantity demanded is at Q_4, whilst the low price leads to less incentive for firms to supply the product, leading to a lower quantity supplied at Q_3. The amount of excess demand is thus $Q_4 - Q_3$.

Eventually, **market forces** will lead to the excess supply or excess demand being resolved. In the case of excess supply, firms will be forced to reduce their prices, leading to a contraction along the supply curve and an extension along the demand curve, eliminating the excess supply and restoring equilibrium at price P_e and quantity Q_e.

In the case of excess demand, firms are able to increase their prices, leading to an extension along the supply curve and a contraction along the demand curve, eliminating the excess demand and restoring equilibrium at price P_e and quantity Q_e.

> **Excess supply**: when the quantity supplied exceeds the quantity demanded, when the price is more than the equilibrium price.
>
> **Excess demand**: when the quantity demanded exceeds the quantity supplied, when the price is less than the equilibrium price.
>
> **Market forces**: also known as the market mechanism — the interaction of the forces of demand and supply.

Now test yourself

TESTED

8 If the current price is above the free market equilibrium price, state whether there is excess demand or excess supply.
9 Explain how equilibrium would eventually be restored by market forces in question 8, above.

Answers on p. 117

Changes in equilibrium price

REVISED

A change in the market equilibrium price may be caused by either a shift of the demand curve or a shift of the supply curve (resulting from a change in the conditions of demand or supply).

An increase in demand

An increase in demand, e.g. for a normal good following an increase in real incomes, would lead to a rightward shift of the demand curve. This would also lead to an increase in equilibrium price and quantity as shown in Figure 2.12.

A decrease in demand

A decrease in demand, e.g. for a normal good following a fall in real incomes, would lead to a leftward shift of the demand curve. This will also lead to a decrease in equilibrium price and quantity as shown in Figure 2.13.

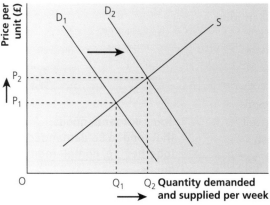

Figure 2.12 An increase in demand

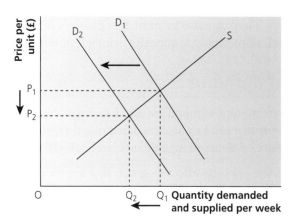

Figure 2.13 A decrease in demand

An increase in supply

An increase in supply, e.g. for coffee following a good harvest, would lead to a rightward shift of the supply curve. This will also lead to a decrease in equilibrium price and an increase in quantity as shown in Figure 2.14.

A decrease in supply

A decrease in supply, e.g. for coffee following a poor harvest, would lead to a leftward shift of the supply curve. This will also lead to an increase in equilibrium price and quantity as shown in Figure 2.15.

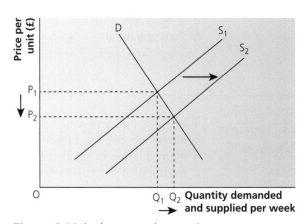

Figure 2.14 An increase in supply

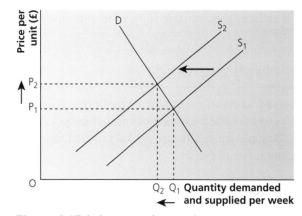

Figure 2.15 A decrease in supply

Now test yourself

TESTED ☐

10 Using a supply and demand diagram in each of the following cases, explain what happens to the equilibrium price and quantity.
   (a) The market for UK seaside holidays following a rise in real incomes.
   (b) The market for copper following the discovery of more efficient mining techniques.
   (c) The market for petrol following the development of new fuel-efficient cars.
   (d) The market for mobile phones following an increase in labour productivity.

Answer on p. 117

The interrelationship between markets

Shifts of demand and supply curves arise not only from changes in market conditions for the product in question, but also from changes in associated markets. They can also be caused by changes of prices of goods in joint demand, joint supply, composite demand, or derived demand.

Joint demand

REVISED

Products in **joint demand** are also known as complementary goods, i.e. goods that tend to be demanded together, such as cars and fuel. Therefore, as demand for cars increases, so will demand for fuel.

This is the opposite effect to goods that are substitutes, or in competing demand, which can be used as an alternative to another good. For example, as demand for cars increases, the demand for public transport may decrease.

> **Joint demand**: goods that tend to be demanded together, i.e. complementary goods.

Joint supply

REVISED

Joint supply exists when the production of one good also leads to the production of another good. An obvious example is the production of beef and leather, both arising from cattle farming.

> **Joint supply**: when the production of one good leads to the production of another good.

Composite demand

REVISED

Composite demand exists when a good is demanded for more than one distinct use. Therefore an increase in the demand for one of the distinct uses reduces the available supply for other uses.

> **Composite demand**: when a good is demanded for more than one distinct use.

Derived demand

REVISED

Derived demand exists when a particular good or factor of production is necessary for the provision of another good or service, e.g. an increase in the demand for healthcare is likely to lead to an increase in the demand for doctors and nurses.

> **Derived demand**: when a particular good or factor of production is necessary for the provision of another good or service.

Now test yourself

TESTED

11 Give an example of each of the following:
   (a) joint demand
   (b) joint supply
   (c) composite demand
   (d) derived demand

12 Which one of the following best describes the relationship between the demand for coach travel and the demand for coach drivers?
   A joint demand
   B complementary demand
   C competitive demand
   D derived demand

Answers on p. 118

Exam practice answers and quick quizzes at **www.hoddereducation.co.uk/myrevisionnotes**

1 The demand curve for games consoles will shift to the right following:
  A a fall in wages of games console manufacturers
  B an increase in indirect tax on games consoles
  C a rise in consumers' real incomes
  D a fall in games console manufacturers' spending on advertising [1]
2 The supply curve for milk will shift to the right following:
  A an increase in advertising by the milk industry
  B a reduction in subsidies to milk producers
  C technological improvements in milk production
  D an increase in population [1]
3 Which of the following would lead to a rise in the price of petrol?
  A improvements in oil extraction technology
  B a reduction in supply of oil from Middle Eastern countries
  C an increase in demand for cars
  D an increase in demand for biofuels [1]
4 The price elasticity of demand for most normal goods is:
  A zero
  B between zero and –1
  C positive
  D negative [1]
5 An increase in the incomes of UK consumers leads to an increase in demand for foreign holidays but a fall in demand for holidays in the UK. The reason for this is:
  A Foreign holidays have a high price elasticity of demand while holidays in the UK have a low price elasticity of demand.
  B There is a negative cross elasticity of demand between foreign holidays and UK holidays.
  C Demand for foreign holidays is income elastic whereas demand for UK holidays is income inelastic.
  D Holidays in the UK are an inferior good while foreign holidays are a normal good. [1]
6 Which of the following would lead to an increase in total revenue?
  A a decrease in the price of a good with price inelastic demand
  B a decrease in the price of a good with price elastic demand
  C an increase in the price of a good with price elastic demand
  D an increase in the price of a good with unitary elastic demand [1]
7 With the help of a diagram, explain what would happen in the market for cars following an increase in the price of petrol. [8]

Answers and quick quizzes online

ONLINE

Summary

You should have an understanding of:
- The meaning of a competitive market.
- The nature of the demand curve.
- The determinants of demand.
- The nature of the supply curve.
- The determinants of supply.
- How to calculate price elasticity of demand and how to interpret the results.
- The factors influencing PED.
- The relationship between PED and total revenue.
- How to calculate income elasticity of demand and how to interpret the results.
- The difference between normal goods and inferior goods.
- How to calculate cross elasticity of demand and how to interpret the results.

- The difference between substitutes and complements.
- How to calculate price elasticity of supply and how to interpret the results.
- The factors influencing price elasticity of supply.
- How changes in price lead to movements along demand and supply curves.
- How changes in the conditions of demand and supply cause shifts of the demand and supply curves for particular products.
- How equilibrium price and quantity is determined.
- Excess demand and excess supply and how market forces will eventually eliminate these disequilibrium situations.
- The possible interrelationships between different markets.

Production and productivity

Production

The term **'production'** refers to the total output of goods and services produced by an individual, firm or country. It also describes the process of converting inputs of raw materials and the services of the various factors of production, such as labour and capital machinery, into outputs.

Productivity

While the term 'production' relates to the total output produced, **productivity** is a measurement of the rate of production by one, or all, of the various factors of production. It is thus a measure of how efficient an individual worker, firm or country is at generating output. Productivity may be defined as the output per factor of production employed per unit of time. If one hairdresser can complete 10 haircuts per day, whilst another can complete 12 in the same time, the latter is more productive. Similarly, if a football striker averages 1.5 goals per game over a season, he or she is more productive than one who averages 0.8 goals per game.

> **Production**: the total output of goods and services produced by an individual, firm or country.
>
> **Productivity**: a measurement of the rate of production by one or more factors of production.
>
> **Labour productivity**: output per worker per unit of time.

Measurement of productivity

The formula for measuring productivity is:

$$\text{Productivity} = \frac{\text{total output per period of time}}{\text{number of units of factor of production}}$$

Thus, the formula for labour productivity would be expressed as:

$$\text{Labour productivity} = \frac{\text{total output per period of time}}{\text{number of units of labour}}$$

Labour costs tend to be the most significant part of total costs for many firms and so **labour productivity** is an important determinant of how competitive firms and individual countries are.

Now test yourself

1 Explain the difference between production and productivity.
2 Calculate the daily productivity of a coffee shop with 3 members of staff who make and sell 450 cups of coffee per day.

Answers on p. 118

Improvements in labour productivity can arise from more and better education and training and from increased motivation. Advances in technology, leading to workers being equipped with the latest capital equipment, can also lead to increased labour productivity. Specialisation and division of labour also facilitate more effective use of specialist capital equipment, which can lead to further increases in labour productivity.

Specialisation, division of labour and exchange

Specialisation

Specialisation involves an individual worker, firm, region or country producing a limited range of goods or services. Examples of specialisation at each level include:

- an individual worker specialising as a tax accountant
- an individual firm specialising in accountancy, e.g. PwC
- an individual region specialising in investment banking, e.g. the City of London
- an individual country specialising in the provision of financial services, e.g. the UK

Division of labour

Specialisation at the level of the individual worker is referred to as the division of labour.

Adam Smith, in his very famous book *The Wealth of Nations*, published in 1776, described the division of labour among groups of workers in a pin factory. Smith argued that, without specialisation, one worker making pins from start to finish might make 20 pins per day, while ten workers specialising in the individual tasks involved might be able to make 48,000 pins per day.

The importance of exchange

Specialisation and the **division of labour** are only viable if an efficient system of **exchange** exists so that, for example, a tax accountant is able to exchange his services for payment so that he can buy food and pay his rent.

Similarly, a country such as the UK can only specialise, to a large extent, in financial services if it is able to exchange this output for other goods and services that it is less able to produce efficiently, such as food and key raw materials.

Throughout most of history, and still in some parts of the world today, exchange has relied upon a system known as barter. Barter involves the exchange of goods and services for other goods and services. A system of exchange involving money as a medium of exchange avoids the need for barter; money also has the benefit of being easily divisible, unlike a particular good.

> **Specialisation**: where an individual worker, firm, region or country produces a limited range of goods or services.
>
> **Division of labour**: specialisation at the level of an individual worker.
>
> **Exchange**: where one thing is traded for something else, e.g. an hour's work is given in return for a set rate of pay.

The benefits of specialisation and division of labour

- Repetition of a limited range of activities can increase skill and aptitude, leading to a worker becoming an expert, e.g. a neurosurgeon.
- Reduced time spent moving between different tasks or workstations means increased productivity.

- As tasks are broken up into smaller ones, it becomes efficient to use specialist machinery.
- Division of labour allows people to work to their natural strengths, for example physical strength, technical skill or the ability to communicate.

Costs of production

Short run versus long run

REVISED

When considering costs of production, economists often distinguish between the **short run** and the **long run** in terms of periods of time. The short run is usually defined as the period of time in which at least one factor of production is fixed in terms of the number of units a firm can use. This helps to define its capacity, or scale of output. In the short run, the most likely factors of production to be fixed are land or capital equipment, while access to labour tends to be more flexible, though not entirely. In the short run, then, firms will have some fixed costs of production for which they must pay even if they do not produce any output, along with variable costs of production that change with the level of output.

In contrast, the long run can be defined as the period of time over which a firm can vary all the factors of production it uses and thus may increase or reduce its scale of output.

> **Short run**: a period of time in which the availability of at least one factor of production is fixed.
>
> **Long run**: a period of time over which all factors of production can be varied.

Fixed and variable costs

REVISED

When an entrepreneur combines the various factors of production to create output and seek a profit, these factors of production incur costs.

Costs are the expenses a business must pay to secure the services of the factors of production and to obtain raw materials. A firm's total costs are made up of fixed costs and variable costs.

Fixed costs

Fixed costs do not vary directly with output in the short run. Examples may include:
- rents on business premises
- buildings insurance
- quarterly heating and lighting bills
- salaries of senior staff
- annual marketing and advertising budget

> **Fixed costs**: costs of production that do not vary with the level of output in the short run.

Average fixed costs (AFC), however, fall as output increases because the firm is able to spread the fixed costs over an increasing volume of output, as shown in Figure 3.1. This is a key incentive for firms to increase their output.

$$AFC = \frac{\text{total fixed costs}}{\text{output}}$$

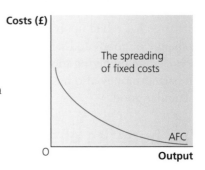

Variable costs

Variable costs are those that vary directly with the level of output. Examples may include:
- raw materials
- packaging

Figure 3.1 Average fixed cost curve slopes downwards

> **Variable costs**: costs of production that vary with the level of output.

- wages of casual staff
- fuel for delivery vehicles
- distribution costs

As shown in Figure 3.2, average variable costs (AVC) initially fall in the short run, but begin to rise at higher levels of output as more units of factors of production (probably labour) begin to overcrowd fixed factors of production. This leads to bottlenecks and disruptions to production. A good analogy here is a busy restaurant kitchen that becomes overcrowded with chefs and other staff; employees get in each other's way, leading to increased wastage and reduced productivity.

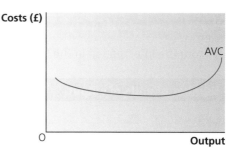

Figure 3.2 **Average variable costs**

$$AVC = \frac{\text{total variable costs}}{\text{output}}$$

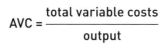

TESTED ☐

> **Exam tip**
>
> Make sure you know the difference between the short run and the long run and between fixed costs and variable costs.

3 Which of the following would be considered a variable cost of production in the short run?
   A heating and lighting
   B building rent
   C salaries of senior staff
   D packaging costs

Answer on p. 118

Total costs (TC)

REVISED ☐

Total costs are made up of total fixed costs and total variable costs of production:

> **Total costs (TC) = total fixed costs (TFC) + total variable costs (TVC)**

Average total costs, or costs per unit of output, are found by dividing total costs by the output being produced:

$$\text{Average total cost (ATC)} = \frac{\text{total costs (TC)}}{\text{output}}$$

And, as shown in Figure 3.3:

> **Average total costs (ATC) = average fixed costs (AFC) + average variable costs (AVC)**

> **Total cost**: the addition of fixed costs and variable costs at a given level of output.
>
> **Average total cost**: total costs of production divided by the number of units of output.

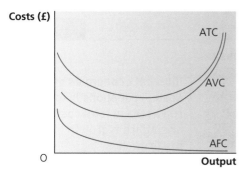

Figure 3.3 **Adding average fixed costs and average variable costs to show average total costs**

4 From the information in the table, what is the total cost of producing 4 units of output?

Number of units of output	Average fixed cost (AFC) (£)	Average variable cost (AVC) (£)
1	60	40
2	30	30
3	20	20
4	15	25

A £40
B £100

C £160
D £200

Answer on p. 118

Economies and diseconomies of scale

Economies of scale

REVISED

Economies of scale are the benefits that can arise as a firm increases its output, leading to reduced average total costs. These cost reductions reflect improvements in productive efficiency. They may give a firm a competitive advantage in the market in which it operates by enabling it to pass on lower prices to consumers and/or generating higher profits that might be re-invested or passed on to shareholders.

> **Economies of scale**: the reduced average total costs that firms experience by increasing output in the long run.

There is a range of potential economies of scale available to firms, depending on the specific features of the industry in which the firm operates, and several may be available at once. For example, the cost of laptop computers has tended to come down steadily as manufacturers such as Apple, HP and Lenovo exploit economies of scale in production and pass these cost savings on to consumers. Figure 3.4 shows that, as a firm increases its output from O in the long run, average costs begin to fall up to output Q_1, due to the effect of one or more economies of scale.

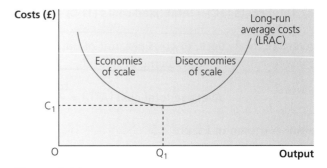

Figure 3.4 Long-run average cost curve

Internal economies of scale

REVISED

Internal economies of scale are those that come about as a result of the growth of the firm itself, and include:
- **Financial economies of scale.** The larger and more reputable a firm is, the more likely it is that banks and other lenders will deem it credit-worthy and a less risky recipient of loan funds. This will lead to it being offered cheaper loans with lower rates of interest, which reduce its costs. On the other hand, smaller, less well-known firms tend not to be able to access the cheapest costs of borrowing, as they are perceived to be more risky. Purchasing economies, where larger firms can take advantage of bulk-buying discounts, are another example of financial economies of scale. This means that firms such as the large

> **Internal economies of scale**: reductions in long-run average total costs arising from growth of the firm.

supermarkets can exert significant buying power when purchasing groceries from suppliers that a smaller, convenience store cannot do.

- **Technical economies of scale.** Larger businesses can generally afford the latest, specialist capital equipment, which is often very expensive. For example, the world's biggest car manufacturing firms such as Toyota and the Volkswagen Group have the financial resources to invest in bespoke assembly lines that increase productivity and reduce average costs of production. A smaller manufacturer such as Aston Martin would not find it cost effective to invest in such technology, so its unit costs are likely to be higher.
- **Marketing economies of scale.** Larger firms are likely to have huge advertising budgets, for example Marks and Spencer's typically lavish TV marketing campaigns around Christmas. However, because of the large volume of sales made by Marks and Spencer, the firm can spread this budget over a larger output than a smaller retailer. This can give larger firms a significant competitive advantage.
- **Managerial economies of scale.** Larger firms can afford to recruit the highest-profile chief executive officers (CEOs) who tend to attract substantial salaries but also tend to be the most effective in increasing profits through a combination of increasing revenues and reducing costs. Furthermore, larger firms can take greater advantage of the division of labour. Large financial services firms, such as PwC, can afford to have specialist managers in areas such as audit, tax and corporate finance, leading to increased productivity and competitive advantage in these areas. A smaller firm of accountants may be forced to provide a more general service, relying on personal service as a source of competitive advantage rather than cost efficiency.

External economies of scale

REVISED

External economies of scale occur when firms benefit from the growth of the industry in which they operate. For example, the development of a successful financial services industry centred on the City of London has meant that firms in London have benefited from easier access to specialised labour and infrastructure, such as transport links to the centre of the financial district.

External economies of scale: reductions in long-run average total costs arising from growth of the industry in which a firm operates.

Diseconomies of scale

REVISED

Diseconomies of scale occur when an increase in a firm's output ceases to yield a reduction in average costs and begins to lead to an increase in average costs of production. This is shown in Figure 3.4 at output levels beyond Q_1. Research suggests several possible sources of diseconomies of scale, arising mainly from problems of managing large businesses:

- **Coordination and control.** As a firm becomes larger, it becomes more difficult to monitor what all resources are doing and how they are deployed. This is likely to lead to increased wastage and loss of quality, leading to increased costs.
- **Communication.** As a firm grows in size, particularly if it is a multinational company operating on different continents in different time zones, it can become difficult to communicate effectively with all offices and staff, leading to ineffective decision making and delays in action. Furthermore, management theory suggests that employees are more likely to feel like 'small fish in a big pond' in larger businesses, leading to a lack of motivation and productivity.

Diseconomies of scale: increases in average total costs that firms may experience by increasing output in the long run.

Exam tip

It is worth being aware of a few examples of very large businesses that have suffered from diseconomies of scale. Large supermarkets and banks have arguably been affected in recent years.

Average revenue, total revenue and profit

Total revenue (TR) and average revenue (AR)

A firm's **total revenue** is found by multiplying price (P) × quantity sold (or demanded) (Q):

Total revenue (TR) = price (P) × quantity (Q)

Figure 3.5 shows how total revenue changes as price changes. At a price of £500, 20 products are demanded per week, giving a total revenue of £10000. If price is reduced to £300, 60 products are demanded per week, giving a total revenue of £18000. In order to calculate **average revenue**, total revenue is divided by the quantity sold:

$$\text{Average revenue (AR)} = \frac{\text{total revenue (TR)}}{\text{quantity (Q)}}$$

Note that average revenue is the same as price, as a simple examination of the above two formulae reveals. Thus the average revenue shows the quantity demanded at each price, which means that the demand curve can also be said to be the average revenue curve.

> **Total revenue**: the money a firm receives from selling its output, calculated by price x quantity sold.
>
> **Average revenue**: total revenue divided by units of output. Equal to price in a firm that sells one product at a fixed price.

5 What is the average revenue of a firm that sells 800 units of a product for a total of £56000?
 A £7
 B £77
 C £70
 D £700

Answer on p. 118

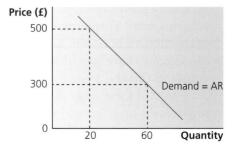

Figure 3.5 Total revenue, average revenue and the demand curve

Profit

Profit is the difference between total revenue and total costs. In other words:

Total profit = total revenue − total costs

If this figure is negative, the firm is making a loss.

Profit is an important driver of business activity because it creates an incentive for entrepreneurs to take a business risk. Economists distinguish between normal profit and supernormal profit. Normal profit is the level of profit required to reward the entrepreneur for taking a risk, while supernormal profit is the profit over and above normal profit, sometimes referred to as excess profit.

> **Profit**: the difference between total revenue and total costs.

> **Typical mistake**
>
> Don't confuse profit with revenue. Profit takes costs away from total revenue.

6 Complete the following table, assuming each football sells for £5 and that variable costs are constant at £2 per unit.

Quantity of footballs sold	Total revenue (£)	Total fixed costs (£)	Total variable costs (£)	Total costs (£)	Profit (£)
10	A	100	H	L	P
20	B	E	I	M	Q
30	C	F	J	N	R
40	D	G	K	O	S

Answer on p. 118

Exam practice

1 Which of the following is most likely to lead to increased labour productivity in an industry?
  A an increase in the number of firms in the industry
  B a reduction in wages paid in the industry
  C an increase in new capital equipment in the industry
  D an increase in demand in the industry [1]

2 Calculate the productivity of the four firms in the following example and complete the table.

Firm	Total output (units)	Number of employees	Productivity (output per employee)
A	140	7	
B	350	25	
C	88	11	
D	261	9	

[4]

3 Explain why specialisation and the division of labour may increase productivity. [4]
4 With the aid of a diagram, explain what happens to a firm's fixed and variable costs in the short run. [6]
5 With the aid of a diagram, explain possible reasons for the shape of a firm's average total cost curve in the long run. [8]
6 Explain how the airline industry might benefit from economies of scale. [8]

Answers and quick quizzes online

ONLINE

Summary

You should have an understanding of:
- The distinction between production and productivity.
- How to calculate labour productivity.
- The meaning of specialisation and the division of labour.
- The need for exchange in allowing for specialisation and division of labour.
- The distinction between the short run and long run in economics.

- The difference between fixed and variable costs of production.
- Economies and diseconomies of scale.
- The difference between internal and external economies of scale.
- Average revenue and total revenue.
- Simple cost and revenue curve diagrams.
- Profit

Market structures

The term **market structure** refers to the number and size of firms within a market for a particular good or service and the extent to which they compete with one another.

Some markets are supplied by a large number of small firms, for example commodities such as wheat. Other markets are supplied by one firm, or a small number of firms, for example internet search engines such as Google.

> **Market structure**: the number and size of firms within a market for a particular good or service.

The spectrum of competition

REVISED

By far the best way to appreciate this idea is to consider the spectrum of competition. As shown in Figure 4.1, this ranges from **perfect competition** at one end to **pure monopoly** at the other end.

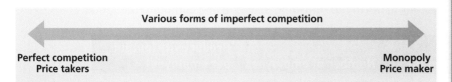

Figure 4.1 A spectrum of competition

In theory, perfect competition is the most competitive form of market structure. Few examples exist of such markets, but the workings of the stock market, or some agricultural markets such as wheat farming, have been considered examples of perfect competition.

Pure monopoly exists when one, and only one, firm supplies the market and it is the least competitive form of market, in theory. Again, there are few examples in reality, although the Royal Mail used to have a legally enforced monopoly for the delivery of letters.

> **Perfect competition**: a market structure that has a large number of buyers and sellers who have perfect information about the market, identical products and few, if any, barriers to entry.
>
> **Imperfect competition**: any market structure that is not perfect competition.
>
> **Pure monopoly**: When only one firm supplies the market.

The objectives of firms

An objective is a target or aim. Firms may have a range of possible objectives.

Profit maximisation

REVISED

The main objective of firms is assumed to be **maximising profit**, i.e. making the maximum positive difference between costs and revenues. A basic assumption of economic theory is that entrepreneurs are encouraged to take business risk and start trading if they believe a profit can be made. There are several benefits to firms of maximising profits. Making large profits can enable firms to:

> **Profit maximisation**: when a firm seeks to make the largest positive difference between total revenue and total costs.

- re-invest funds into developing new products that lead to them to gain more customers
- pay out higher returns to shareholders which may encourage more people to buy shares in the company, or help boost the share price

> **Exam tip**
>
> Unless told otherwise, assume that the primary objective of firms in economic theory is to maximise profits.

Sales maximisation

REVISED

This occurs when firms' sales revenue is at a maximum. Sales maximisation occurs at the level of output at which the sale of one more unit would not add to overall revenue. This can help the firm benefit from economies of scale.

> **Exam tip**
>
> Don't confuse profit maximisation with sales revenue maximisation.

Survival

REVISED

A large proportion of new businesses fail in the first few years of operation. In its early stages of life, therefore, a key objective of a firm might simply be to survive the critical period before it establishes a customer base and repeat sales, and is able to cover its costs.

Growth

REVISED

Once a firm has survived the critical first few years of its life, its owners are likely to pursue an objective of growth. This will involve a firm increasing its output and scale of operations, possibly in terms of expanding its productive base and the size of its workforce. Growth means that a firm may be able to take advantage of various economies of scale outlined earlier in Chapter 3. This objective will also help a business fend off any takeover bids from rival companies.

Increasing market share

REVISED

Linked to the objective of growth is one of **increasing market share**. Having the highest market share for a particular product can give a firm the benefits of monopoly power outlined later in this chapter, although this may also attract attention from the government, which may fear that such firms could abuse their power.

> **Increasing market share**: when a firm seeks to maximise its percentage share of a market in terms of sales value or number of units sold.

Stakeholder objectives

REVISED

The preceding objectives assume that all firms are predominantly interested in achieving financial objectives. A more modern view is that firms may achieve financial and non-financial objectives at the same time. Firms are seen to be looking to satisfy the needs of a range of business **stakeholders**. Firms may take the view, for example, that looking after the needs of their employees is at least as important as maximising profit. If there is a genuine commitment to doing this, this may show the firm in a good light, which may lead to it being seen as a good place to work.

> **Stakeholder**: any individual or group with an interest in how a business is run.

1 A newly started business is most likely to aim for which of the following objectives in the short run?
   A   sales maximisation   C   survival
   B   stakeholder objectives   D   growth

Answer on p. 118

Competitive markets

Understanding perfect competition   REVISED

'Perfect' does not necessarily mean 'best' in this sense. It means an extremely competitive market, made up of a large number of small firms, with each firm being too small to influence the market price on its own. Indeed, firms which exist in a perfectly competitive market are described as **price takers**, since they are obliged by market forces to accept the market equilibrium price, or risk going out of business.

> **Price taker**: a firm that is unable to influence the ruling market price and thus has to accept it.

Assumptions of perfect competition include:
- few, if any, barriers to entry to a market
- consumers and firms have complete, or perfect, knowledge of all the products supplied by firms, as well as their prices
- products are identical, or homogeneous

The impact of these features is that any firm that tries to sell its product at a price higher than the market equilibrium will not make any sales, since consumers will know about the cheaper alternatives and, since all products are identical, have no loyalty to any particular firm. Therefore all firms must accept the market price if they are to remain in the market.

Price determination in highly competitive markets   REVISED

We can show how perfect competition works using supply and demand analysis, shown in Figure 4.2.

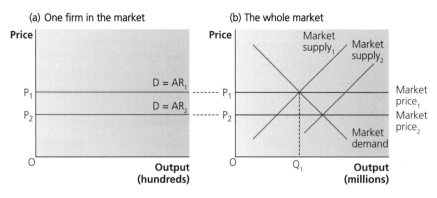

Figure 4.2 Price determination in highly competitive markets

Figure 4.2(b) shows a highly competitive market, with firms supplying this market earning supernormal profits. Initial market equilibrium price is P_1 and market output is Q_1. This leads to each individual firm facing price P_1, as in Figure 4.2(a). Because of the key features of highly competitive markets, if other firms become aware that the existing firms in the market are earning supernormal profits, which they can easily do because of the existence of perfect information, they will enter the market easily due to the low, possibly non-existent barriers to entry.

This will have the effect of increasing overall supply in the market, as shown in Figure 4.2(b), which leads to a rightward shift of the market supply curve. This reduces the equilibrium price to P_2 as output increases beyond Q_1. This increase in supply and reduction in price will occur up to the point at which only normal profit is made, meaning that only the most competitive firms survive in the market.

Advantages of perfect competition

REVISED ☐

Economists usually agree that a highly competitive market functions well in 'static' terms, achieving productive and allocative efficiency.

● **Productive efficiency.** Highly competitive markets help to achieve productive efficiency. This occurs when goods and services are produced at minimum average cost, or when minimum inputs are used to produce maximum outputs. Any firm that does not achieve this will lose its market share to rival firms which can produce the same product more cheaply. For example, in the market for barbers, where few barriers to entry exist and there is little to differentiate one from another, any barber that does not minimise its costs and hence price is likely to struggle to retain customers.
● **Allocative efficiency.** Highly competitive markets will lead to firms producing what consumers demand since, if they do not, they will lose market share to firms that are producing the most desired products. This leads to consumer sovereignty, i.e. the consumer is 'king' (or queen!). Again, in the market for barbers, if a supplier does not offer haircuts that customers desire at a competitive price then it will lose sales to rival barbers.

Productive and allocative efficiency are the components of **static efficiency**, i.e. efficiency measured at a point in time.

> **Static efficiency**: efficiency measured at a point in time, comprising productive efficiency and allocative efficiency.

Monopoly and monopoly power

Monopoly

REVISED ☐

A pure monopoly exists when there is a single supplier of a good or service, which therefore has 100% market share. As with perfect competition, there are few examples of pure monopoly in reality. Economists study these theoretical models in order to examine the performance of firms in real life compared with these extreme examples. Tesco, with a market share in the groceries market of around 30%, and Google, with a market share of around 90% of internet traffic, may be considered monopolies in the UK.

Monopoly power

A firm need not have a pure monopoly in order to exert **monopoly power** and there are many industries dominated by a small number of firms with monopoly power. In such industries, barriers to entry to the market will tend to be high. Firms with monopoly power can restrict their output in order to raise price, which boosts their supernormal profits. Because of barriers to entry, firms are able to maintain these profits because it is unlikely that new firms can easily enter the market to compete the profits away. This is shown in Figure 4.3.

> **Monopoly power**: the power of a firm in a market to act as a price maker.
>
> **Price maker**: a firm with the power to set the ruling market price.

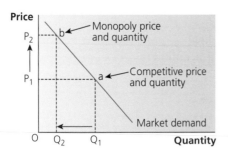

Figure 4.3 **A firm with monopoly power restricts output to raise price**

Barriers to entry

Barriers to entry are features of a market that make it difficult for new firms to enter that market and can therefore lead to monopoly power. There are several possible barriers to entry, which include the following.

> **Barrier to entry**: any feature of a market that makes it difficult or impossible for new firms to enter.

Natural barriers to entry

These may include naturally occurring climatic, geographical or geological factors that make the product difficult to replicate elsewhere. For example, it is said that the soil and weather around Reims and Epernay in northern France are ideal for the production of the grape varieties that are combined to make champagne. Therefore other sparkling wines do not have the same exclusivity.

Economies of scale

Economies of scale occur when a firm's average costs of production fall as output increases. These mean that large firms can set their prices below those of any potential new entrant firms to the market, and still make a supernormal profit. For example, a large supermarket such as Tesco will be able to negotiate a much cheaper price per unit when buying dairy products from farmers in terms of a bulk-buying discount, than a much smaller, independent convenience store. This acts as a deterrent for new firms to enter the market.

Legal barriers

These include patents, copyrights and trademarks and essentially give a single firm or individual the right to have a monopoly over a new product, process or other intellectual property either forever or over a given time. For example, the British inventor James Dyson holds many patents over his original designs for a range of household appliances, most notably vacuum cleaners, which cannot legally be copied.

Product differentiation

Existing firms in a market may have spent considerable sums of money over many years on advertising and branding in order to build up a significant consumer loyalty and marketing profile — the process of **product differentiation**. For example, it would be extremely difficult for any new cola manufacturer to take market share from Coca-Cola and PepsiCo. Both firms have spent billions of dollars over many years on advertising, including the sponsorship of major sporting events such as the football World Cup and American Super Bowl.

> **Product differentiation**: using advertising or product design to make a product seem different from those of competitors.

Sunk costs

Sunk costs are the costs that cannot easily be recovered if a firm is unsuccessful in a market and has to exit, i.e. these financial commitments are essentially lost, or 'sunk'. Such costs may include spending on specialist market research or specialist equipment that could not easily be sold to another firm. For example, an oil company may have to spend many millions of pounds on detecting resources of crude oil before it begins to extract any. The threat of losing this money acts as a deterrent to new firms considering entering a market.

> **Sunk costs**: costs that cannot easily be recovered if a firm is unsuccessful in a market and has to exit.

Now test yourself

TESTED ☐

3 Which of the following may create a barrier to entry?
  A   two small firms merging in a large industry
  B   a government granting exclusive rights to a firm to run a rail franchise on a major route
  C   a firm cutting its price in a highly competitive market
  D   the setting up of a price comparison website

Answer on p. 118

Concentrated markets

REVISED ☐

Monopolies and **oligopolies** (close to monopoly on the spectrum of competition) may be considered **concentrated markets**, i.e. markets dominated by a small number of firms. It is possible to calculate the degree of concentration that exists by using the **concentration ratio**. This is equal to the total market share held by the largest firms in a market.

> **Oligopoly**: a market structure dominated by a small number of powerful firms.
>
> **Concentrated market**: a market dominated by a small number of firms.
>
> **Concentration ratio**: a measurement of how concentrated a market is — the total market share held by the largest firms in a market.

Now test yourself

TESTED ☐

4 Which of the following would be a consequence of a perfectly competitive market being replaced by a monopoly?
  A   Lower price and higher output
  B   Higher price and restricted output
  C   Lower profit
  D   Lower barriers to entry

Answer on p. 118

Advantages and disadvantages of monopoly

REVISED ☐

If perfect competition leads, in theory at least, to desirable outcomes in terms of productive and allocative efficiency, this implies that monopolies are undesirable. Indeed, in theory, there is a range of potential disadvantages of firms holding monopoly power. However, there are many examples of industries dominated by a small number of large firms and so there must also be potential advantages of monopolies to society.

Disadvantages of monopoly

There are some potential disadvantages of monopoly, which the government would take into account when deciding whether or not a large firm is operating in the public's best interests.

Productive and allocative inefficiency

As you saw in Chapter 3, productive efficiency occurs when firms produce at minimum average total cost, i.e. when minimum inputs are used to produce maximum outputs. If it is assumed that monopolies do not have to be competitive to survive, because they do not face the threat of firms taking their market share and so there is little incentive (other than generating profits for shareholders) to cut costs to a minimum. Allocative efficiency occurs when firms produce products that consumers value most highly, in the right quantities. Because monopolies do not have to produce the 'best' goods and services, because there are few, if any, competitors, consumers may have little choice but to buy whatever is produced. This would be allocatively inefficient.

Diseconomies of scale

Diseconomies of scale exist when a firm's average costs of production begin to increase as it expands its output. Very large firms may suffer from problems of control or communication. In a multinational company that operates across time zones and languages, the company's operations may be so vast that it is difficult to coordinate every employee and product line.

Possible advantages of monopoly

There must be some possible benefits arising from the existence of monopolies, or they would surely be outlawed.

Economies of scale

One of the main advantages of monopoly is a range of potential economies of scale, which means that as a firm increases its output, its average costs of production fall. Such economies of scale could be:
- financial
- technical
- related to marketing
- managerial

Innovation

Since firms in concentrated markets such as monopolies make supernormal profits, there is arguably more funding available to invest in research and development, leading to **innovation** and better-quality products. This is the argument in favour of granting legal monopolies in the form of patents to large pharmaceutical companies: if they could not make supernormal profits, they might argue, people's quality of life might suffer due to a lack of new medicines and vaccines.

> **Innovation**: new products and production processes that are developed into marketable goods or services.

Exam practice answers and quick quizzes at **www.hoddereducation.co.uk/myrevisionnotes**

5 Which of the following is a potential benefit to consumers of a monopoly?
   A   allocative efficiency
   B   perfect information
   C   supernormal profit
   D   innovation

Answer on p. 118

Natural monopoly

REVISED

One special case, which is another argument in favour of concentrated markets, is that of a **natural monopoly**. This is where it is uneconomic for more than one firm to supply a market because a firm enjoys continuous economies of scale.

> **Natural monopoly**: a market where a single firm can benefit from continuous economies of scale.

Examples often used are the utilities markets, such as household gas, electricity and water. Using the language of economists, the supply infrastructure of these markets most closely fits the concept of a natural monopoly. For example, if more than one firm were responsible for supplying gas pipelines to homes and businesses, roads would be constantly dug up when users changed their supplier. As it is, effectively just one firm (Transco) deals with the pipeline aspect of gas supply, but allows other energy billing companies, such as E.ON and npower, to use the pipelines to supply the gas itself to homes and businesses. It is productively efficient for just a single firm to supply the market, as several individual firms could never achieve the low costs of the single firm.

In a natural monopoly, firms experience continuous economies of scale, which means that as they increase their output, their average costs of production continue to fall. This implies that if the market were broken into more than one firm, average costs would be higher than for a single firm, meaning that prices might have to be higher.

The competitive market process

How firms in concentrated markets behave

REVISED

Price competition

Firms in concentrated markets are likely to benefit from economies of scale, which reduce their average costs of production such that firms may be able to reduce prices while still being able to make a supernormal profit.

> **Price competition**: reducing the price of a good or service in order to make it more attractive than those of competitors.

These firms may, as we have seen, also be able to make use of these profits to re-invest into research and development in order to come up with new, innovative products and methods of production. This can lead to a **dynamic efficiency** which leads to a reduction in the firms' costs at every given output level. Again, this can allow firms to reduce prices while still being able to make a supernormal profit.

> **Dynamic efficiency**: improvement in productive efficiency over time.

If a firm wishes to take market share from rivals, it may initiate a **price war**, whereby one firm begins by undercutting others. This will, however, tend to reduce the profits earned by all firms and is therefore often only used as a last resort.

> **Price war**: where firms in an industry repeatedly cut prices below those of competitors in order to win market share.

Non-price competition

Firms in highly concentrated markets compete vigorously on the basis of factors other than price. This is because any attempt by one firm to undercut the prices of its rivals may spark extreme price competition — a price war — which can damage the profits of all firms involved. For example, quality of service can attract customers to give a firm repeat business. A number of major car retailers pride themselves on high-quality after-sales service to maintain a strong consumer loyalty. Similarly, the major supermarkets make extensive use of customer loyalty cards. In return for exchanging commercially valuable information with the supermarket, consumers build up points that give special offers.

> **Non-price competition**: competition on the basis of product features other than price, such as quality, advertising or after-sales service.

Exam practice

1 Explain two reasons why you think some firms may seek objectives other than profit maximisation. [4]
2 Identify four main features of perfectly competitive markets. [4]
3 With the help of a diagram, explain how price is determined in a competitive market. [8]
4 Using a supply and demand diagram, explain what would happen in the market for wheat following the entry of several new firms. [8]
5 With the help of a diagram, explain how price is determined in a concentrated market. [8]
6 Using the table, calculate the market share of the top five firms in the UK banking market. [2]

Market shares held by selected high street banks in the UK, 2014

Bank	Market share (%)
Lloyds	15.6
Barclays	13.2
NatWest	11.4
HSBC	11.2
Santander	10.1
Halifax	9.1
Nationwide	6.2
Bank of Scotland	4.2
Royal Bank of Scotland	3.8
Co-operative Bank	2.1

Source: GfK/NOP

7 (a) How would you expect existing firms in a highly concentrated market such as petrol stations to behave? [4]
  (b) How might the existing firms respond to the threat of a potential new competitor? [4]

Answers and quick quizzes online

ONLINE

Summary

You should have an understanding of:
- The meaning of market structure.
- The main types of market structure.
- The features of competitive markets and perfect competition.
- The features of concentrated markets and monopoly.
- Monopoly and monopoly power.
- Objectives of firms, such as profit maximisation.

- How prices are determined in competitive markets.
- How prices are determined in monopoly markets.
- How barriers to entry influence market structure.
- Concentration ratios.
- How firms in concentrated markets compete on the basis of price and non-price methods.

How markets and prices allocate resources

The functions of prices

The price mechanism has four key functions in a free market economy:

1 **The rationing function:** as prices rise, excess demand is removed and only those consumers with the ability to pay are able to purchase the good.

2 **The signalling function:** prices provide important market signals to market participants, e.g. to producers to either increase or decrease production.

3 **The incentive function:** increased prices strengthen incentives to firms to produce more in order to make a profit.

4 **The allocative function:** the allocative function acts to divert resources to where they can maximise their returns and away from uses where they do not.

When any of these key functions of prices breaks down, market failure is said to occur.

> **Rationing function:** increasing prices rations demand to those most able to afford a good or service.
>
> **Signalling function:** prices provide important information to market participants.
>
> **Incentive function:** prices create incentives for market participants to change their actions.
>
> **Allocative function:** the function of prices that acts to divert resources to where returns can be maximised.

Now test yourself

1 The rationing function of prices means that:

A Changes in prices provide information to producers and consumers about changes in demand and supply.

B An increase in prices will encourage more firms to enter an industry.

C When there is a shortage of a product, prices will rise and put some consumers off buying the product.

D A rise in price will worsen any shortage of a product.

Answer on p. 118

The meaning of market failure

Market failure occurs whenever a market leads to a misallocation of resources — in other words, when a market fails to achieve productive efficiency, allocative efficiency or equity.

Market failure can be complete or partial. **Complete market failure** occurs when the free market fails to create a market for a good or service (i.e. a missing market). A prime example would be for so-called 'public goods' such as lighthouses, since everybody would have an incentive to wait for somebody else to provide them. **Partial market failure** arises when a market exists, but does not provide resources in the optimum quantities, i.e. there is either over-production/consumption or under-production/consumption of a good or service.

> **Market failure:** when the free market leads to a misallocation of resources in an economy.
>
> **Complete market failure:** when the free market fails to create a market for a good or service, also referred to as a missing market.
>
> **Partial market failure:** when a market for a good or service exists, but it is consumed or produced in quantities that do not maximise economic welfare.

TESTED ☐

2 Partial market failure exists when:
   A   A product is both non-excludable and non-rival.
   B   There is excess supply in a market at the current market price.
   C   A market exists but there is under-production.
   D   The market can only be competitive with government subsidies.

Answer on p. 118

Public goods, private goods and quasi-public goods

Public goods are those that possess two key characteristics: they are **non-excludable** and **non-rival**.

- **Non-excludable** means that non-paying customers cannot be excluded from consuming a good, once it has been produced. For example, once a lighthouse has emitted its beam of light, all ships in the vicinity can use this light to avoid rocks and other hazards at sea.
- **Non-rival** means that one person's enjoyment of the good does not diminish another person's enjoyment of the good. For example, one person listening to a radio broadcast does not diminish the quality of radio signal to any other listener.

Public good: a good that is non-excludable and non-rival in consumption.

Non-excludable: where it is not possible to prevent non-paying customers from consuming a good.

Non-rival: where one person's enjoyment of a good does not diminish another person's enjoyment of the good.

Now test yourself TESTED ☐

3 A good is non-excludable if:
   A   its price is zero
   B   it is supplied by the government rather than the free market
   C   it is not possible to prevent non-paying customers from enjoying it
   D   one person's use affects the quantity available for others

Answer on p. 118

The free-rider problem   REVISED ☐

Public goods are an example of complete market failure, as the free market would have no incentive to provide them. For example, in the case of sea defences such as flood protection, coastal homeowners would have an incentive to wait for their neighbours or others in a similar situation to fund the flood protection and thus it will not be provided at all. This is referred to as the free-rider problem, since individual consumers hope to get a 'free ride' without paying for the benefit they enjoy.

Private goods   REVISED ☐

Private goods are the opposite of public goods, i.e. they are both excludable and rival. This means that non-payers can be excluded from consuming a good and consumption by one person diminishes the enjoyment of the good by another. For example, if you eat a slice of pizza, another person cannot also enjoy that slice.

Private good: a good that is rival and excludable in consumption.

Quasi-public goods

REVISED

Quasi- (or near) **public goods** are those that possess some, but not all, characteristics of a public good. For example, they may be partially excludable, or partially rival. Depending on location and time of day, roads may be considered private goods, quasi-public goods or public goods.

> **Quasi-public good**: a good which exhibits some, but not all, of the characteristics of a public good, i.e. it is partially non-excludable and/or partially non-rival.

Externalities

REVISED

Externalities are the knock-on effects of economic transactions upon third parties. There are many instances where the actions of individual consumers or producers have consequences that affect others.

> **Externality**: a knock-on effect of an economic transaction upon third parties.

Positive externalities in production

REVISED

Positive externalities in production occur when the actions of firms have wider benefits to society. For example, when a new airport runway is built there may be positive knock-on effects in terms of increased tourism revenue to UK firms and an increased attractiveness to the UK for foreign investment. In this case, it is said that the **private costs** to the firm are greater than the costs to society, as shown in Figure 5.1.

> **Positive externality**: A positive knock-on effect of an economic transaction upon third parties, also known as an external benefit.
>
> **Private cost**: the cost to an individual producer involved in a market transaction.

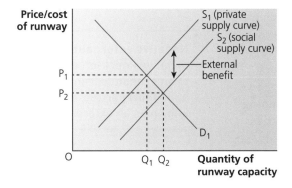

Figure 5.1 Positive externalities in production

The private costs in this case are given by supply curve S_1 while **social costs** are given by supply curve S_2. The vertical distance between the two supply curves shows the external benefit from the building of the runway. The free market quantity of runway capacity would be Q_1, at price P_1. The free market would thus lead to underproduction of Q_2-Q_1 as the free market would be unlikely to take into account the full benefits to society.

> **Social cost**: the total of private cost plus external cost of an economic transaction.

Positive externalities in consumption

REVISED

Positive externalities in consumption occur when the actions of an individual consumer have positive knock-on impacts on others in society, i.e. external benefits arise. An individual who adopts a healthy lifestyle and gets regular medical check-ups may be expected to take fewer days off work through illness and be more productive than somebody who does not. As such, they may require less overall government health spending over the course of their lives and may contribute to a higher standard of living for the nation as a whole. In such cases, **social benefits** exceed **private benefits**, as shown in

> **Social benefit**: the total of private benefit plus external benefit of an economic transaction.
>
> **Private benefit**: the benefit to an individual consumer involved in a market transaction.

Figure 5.2. In a free market with no government intervention, there will be under-consumption of goods with positive externalities. In other words, demand is too low. There is overlap with the concept of a merit good.

In the diagram, demand curve D$_1$ reflects the private benefits of exercise and a healthy lifestyle. However, the full benefits to society of all citizens pursuing a healthy lifestyle, shown by demand curve D$_2$, are not fully appreciated and thus there is under-consumption of Q$_2$–Q$_1$.

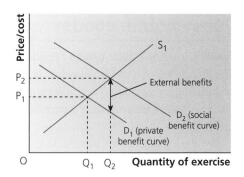

Figure 5.2 Positive externalities in consumption

Now test yourself

TESTED

4 Positive externalities are present if:
  A   social costs exceed private costs
  B   private benefits exceed private costs
  C   production leads to private benefits
  D   private benefits are less than social benefits

Answer on p. 118

Negative externalities in production

REVISED

Negative externalities in production may arise if a firm fails to take into account the wider negative impacts of their activities upon society, i.e. there are external costs. A coastal oil refinery not obliged to account for its wider impact may pollute the atmosphere and local beaches with its emissions and waste products. This will clearly have negative consequences for groups beyond the owners of the factory, including health and environmental consequences. In these situations, social costs exceed the private costs of production (such as raw materials and wages). The market failure arises because output is greater than the social optimum and the price is too low to take full account of all costs of production, including external costs, as shown in Figure 5.3.

> **Negative externality**: a negative knock-on effect of an economic transaction upon third parties, also known as an external cost.

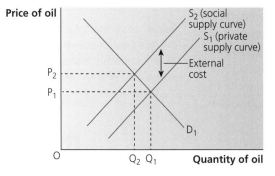

Figure 5.3 Negative externalities in production

Negative externalities in consumption

REVISED

In this situation individuals consume 'too much' of a product, as shown in Figure 5.4, and the benefits to the individual consumer exceed the benefits to society. In the case of goods such as less-healthy foods, alcohol, tobacco and drugs, individual consumers/users fail to appreciate that society may not benefit as much from their consumption. Indeed, **information failure** may explain some of the over-consumption of such goods if people become intoxicated or addicted and less able to make 'rational' decisions. Thus there is overlap with the concept of demerit goods.

> **Information failure**: a source of market failure where market participants do not have enough information to be able to make effective judgements about the 'correct' levels of consumption or production of a good.

> **Exam tip**
>
> Make sure you can draw accurate diagrams to illustrate positive and negative externalities.

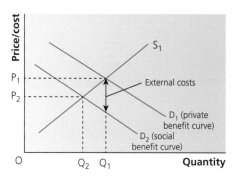

Figure 5.4 **Negative externalities in consumption**

Now test yourself — TESTED

5 Which of the products below has a market price which most accounts for negative externalities?

Product	Private cost per unit (£)	External cost per unit (£)	Market price (£)
A	15	5	16
B	20	2	22
C	12	10	13
D	16	7	21

Answer on p. 118

Merit and demerit goods

> **Merit good**: a good that would be under-consumed in a free market.
>
> **Demerit good**: a good that would be over-consumed in a free market.

Sometimes, society judges that some goods or services are either under-consumed or over-consumed. Goods that are under-consumed in a free market are known as **merit goods**, while those that would be over-consumed are known as **demerit goods**. 'Under-consumption' and 'over-consumption' in this sense are normative, subjective terms that involve value judgements being made by the governments of the countries concerned.

Merit goods

REVISED

Classic examples of merit goods include education and healthcare, though several other goods and services may fit the criteria outlined below, including:
● exercise
● car insurance
● healthy foods

There is some overlap between the concepts of a merit good and a positive externality in consumption.

Merit goods would be under-consumed in a free market, for several possible reasons:

● People are not aware of the potential private benefits to themselves from consuming the merit good, especially in the long term. In the case of education, it is very difficult for some individuals to appreciate fully the benefits to themselves from attending school or college for several years; it can be hard to see the relevance of parts of a standard curriculum to their daily lives. This is an example of information failure, which means that one, or both, parties to an economic transaction do not possess all the information they need to make an accurate decision, or they are not aware of how to use the information available. In terms of education, people may not see personal benefits such as increased productivity and employability, leading to higher earnings over the course of their lifetime.

● People may not be able to afford the product. It would cost an individual several thousands of pounds per person per year to fund their own education and many would not be able to afford this.

● People may not take into account the wider benefits to society of their use of merit goods. These wider benefits can be seen as positive externalities and may include, in the case of education, a greater overall standard of living for society as a result of higher output and increased innovation. Individual consumers are not, however, required to take these into account.

Now test yourself

TESTED

6 A merit good, such as education is:
  A   non-excludable with positive externalities in production
  B   non-rival with positive externalities in consumption
  C   rival with positive externalities in production only
  D   excludable with positive externalities in consumption

Answer on p. 118

Demerit goods

REVISED

Demerit goods include 'recreational' drugs, such as alcohol and tobacco, and other aspects of an unhealthy lifestyle such as fatty, sugary foods. Demerit goods are those that would be over-consumed in a free market, and often give rise to negative externalities in consumption.

Demerit goods are over-consumed for a number of reasons:

● People may not be aware of the damage to their health arising from consumption. For example, in the case of smoking cigarettes, people are not aware of, or choose to ignore, the various smoking-related illnesses. This is another example of information failure.

● Goods are too cheap and so people can too easily afford them, or they are too accessible. For example, some people are concerned that strong alcohol is too cheap and too easily available, even to the under-aged.

● Individuals do not take account of the wider external costs associated with their consumption. For example, cigarette smoking by one person may inflict health damage on others in the vicinity. Similarly, excessive drinking by certain groups may lead to antisocial behaviour, which may create noise or other disturbance to others outside the group.

Market imperfections

Economists often make use of theoretical 'perfect' markets in order to make comparisons with markets in reality. Perfect markets have the following features:

- perfect information
- no barriers to entry and exit
- homogeneous products and factors of production
- large numbers of buyers and sellers
- perfect mobility of factors of production

These features are clearly unrealistic and real-life markets tend to have a range of imperfections as outlined below.

Imperfect and asymmetric information

REVISED

Imperfect information exists when economic agents (consumers, employees, producers or government) do not know everything they need to know in order to make a fully informed decision. Individual consumers may not be fully aware of the positive and negative consequences of their use of certain goods, especially in the long term. As a result they may consume insufficient or excessive amounts in terms of maximising the overall welfare of society.

Asymmetric information is a similar concept but implies that one economic agent knows more than another, giving that agent more power in the decision-making process. A good example of this is in the market for second-hand cars, where the seller often knows whether or not the car is in full working order. Unless the buyer knows what he or she is looking for, the only signal they may have as to the quality of the car is the price. Being aware of this, the seller will price good and bad examples of the same car at similar prices, making it even more difficult for uninformed buyers to make favourable decisions. Unscrupulous producers may thus exploit consumers. Appropriate government intervention here may be designed to improve the quality and reliability of information held by economic agents, and to redress the imbalance in the case of asymmetric information.

> **Imperfect information**: when economic agents do not know everything they need to know in order to make a fully informed decision.
>
> **Asymmetric information**: a source of information failure where one economic agent knows more than another, giving them more power in a market transaction.

Monopoly

REVISED

Monopoly is an extreme example of a market structure that, in its pure form, means that only one firm supplies a market. In a free market without government intervention, a monopoly producer has no incentive to be economically efficient, since there are no rival firms to take its market share. This is because of significant barriers to entry to the market, such as product differentiation and large economies of scale. This means that consumers will not benefit from the lowest prices, or have a choice of products. Thus the market failure leads to productive and allocative inefficiency and possibly reduced choice for consumers, an equity issue.

Now test yourself

7 A highly competitive market is taken over by a monopoly producer. This may result in:
   A   lower costs
   B   lower prices
   C   lower profits
   D   lower research and development

Answer on p. 118

Immobility of factors of production

Factors of production, especially labour, are unlikely to be perfectly mobile between different uses or occupations. For example, a former steel worker may not find it easy to switch quickly to working as an IT consultant, since he or she may lack the specific skills and qualifications required. This is referred to as **occupational immobility**.

In addition, individuals may not be aware of, or easily able to move to, where jobs exist. For example, an IT consultant currently living and working in the north of England may not be able to afford accommodation in London or the southeast of the country, and so may not be able to obtain a promotion in their field of work. It is also possible that they have dependent relatives in their current location and so may not wish to leave their home city. This would lead to **geographical immobility**.

> **Occupational immobility**: a source of factor immobility that means workers find it difficult to move between occupations for reasons of lack of desirable skills.
>
> **Geographical immobility**: a source of factor immobility that means workers have difficulty in moving to locations where jobs are available for reasons such as a lack of affordable housing or family commitments.

Now test yourself

8 Which one of the following is most likely to lead to immobility of labour?
   A   government subsidising training courses
   B   regional differences in house prices
   C   improved information about job availability
   D   government subsidising public transport

Answer on p. 118

An inequitable distribution of income and wealth

Equity is the notion of fairness in the allocation of economic resources. In a market economy, with no government intervention, those individuals with the greatest ability to pay, i.e. the highest incomes, will tend to have access to the greatest share of resources.

Different economies around the world and over time have taken a range of views about what level of inequality is acceptable. Free market capitalists would argue that inequality creates useful incentives among economic agents that positively influence overall national income and can 'trickle down' to poorer members of society, raising overall living standards. Critics of free market capitalism might say that inequality creates social tensions between the relatively rich and poor, leading to reduced living standards.

> **Equity**: the notion of fairness in society.
>
> **Inequitable distribution of income and wealth**: when the way in which income and wealth are distributed in society is considered unfair.

Government intervention in markets

Reasons for government intervention

The free market often fails to achieve an efficient or equitable allocation of resources. Cases such as over-consumption of certain demerit goods and the potential hiking of prices by monopoly firms provide justification for some form or forms of intervention.

However, reasons for government intervention are not solely microeconomic. The government has important wider macroeconomic objectives that are focused on improving the overall performance of the UK economy and living standards for the population as a whole.

So the main reasons for government intervention are to:
- correct any market failure
- achieve a fairer (or more equitable) distribution of income and wealth
- achieve the government's macroeconomic objectives for the economy

Indirect taxation

Governments can use **indirect taxes** to alter the supply of certain goods or services. Indirect taxes have the effect of increasing the costs of firms, which means they lead to the supply curve shifting leftwards.

The government can use two different types of indirect taxation:
1 **Specific, or unit taxes** — these involve a fixed amount being added per unit of a good or service, such as that on bottles of alcohol.
2 *Ad valorem* **taxes** — these involve adding a percentage of the price of a good or service, for example VAT at 20% would add 20p to a product costing £1, but £20 to a product costing £100.

> **Indirect tax**: a tax on spending, sometimes used to reduce consumption of demerit goods.

The impacts of the two different types of indirect tax are shown in Figure 5.5.

Advantages of using indirect taxation

Indirect taxes are often placed on goods that have inelastic demand. This means that strong tax revenues can be gained for governments, which can then be assigned to specific areas of spending, such as healthcare.

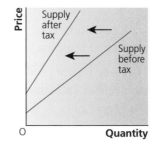
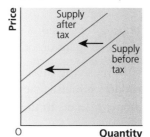

Figure 5.5 Indirect taxation shifting a supply curve

Use of the price mechanism leaves it up to consumers and producers to decide how to adjust their behaviour.

Assuming governments have applied the correct rate of taxation, the tax helps to internalise an external cost, i.e. to reflect more accurately the impact of a negative externality on price and quantity.

Disadvantages of using indirect taxation

Because indirect taxes are often placed on inelastic goods, the quantity demanded may not fall very much unless the tax is very large, which reduces the impact of the tax.

In practice, it can be extremely difficult to place an accurate monetary value on external costs, which makes it almost impossible to correctly 'internalise' a negative externality.

Indirect taxes tend to be regressive in nature, which means they take a larger percentage of a poorer person's income. This may be seen as unfair.

UK firms may be concerned that their international competitiveness may be reduced by the imposition of indirect taxes, which increase their production costs relative to those of foreign competitors.

Subsidies

REVISED

Subsidies are government grants paid to producers to encourage increased production of certain goods or services, such as merit goods. By reducing the price of specific goods or services, the government is also attempting to increase their consumption. Subsidies can also be used to promote the use of products which reduce external costs, such as public transport. Granting a government subsidy has the effect of shifting the supply curve to the right.

> **Subsidy**: a payment made to producers to encourage increased production of a good or service.

The impact of a subsidy is shown in Figure 5.6.

Advantages of using subsidies

Subsidies on merit goods can increase their consumption, bringing the equilibrium quantity closer to the social optimum, helping to internalise the external benefit.

Subsidies reduce the price of a good, making it more affordable for those on lower incomes, so reducing the effects of relative poverty.

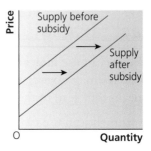

Figure 5.6 A subsidy shifting a supply curve

Disadvantages of using subsidies

As in the case of taxing negative externalities, it is extremely difficult in practice to place an accurate monetary value on the size of external benefits.

Funding for subsidies carries an opportunity cost, i.e. the money could have been spent on other things such as building new hospitals or roads.

Firms receiving subsidies may become reliant on them, encouraging productive inefficiency and laziness, and reducing international competitiveness in the long run.

Subsidies for UK firms may be viewed by foreign governments as a form of artificial trade protection, encouraging them to retaliate by erecting their own forms of protection.

If subsidies are placed on goods or services with inelastic demand, they may reduce price but not significantly increase consumption.

Now test yourself

TESTED

9 A government subsidy:
   A   leads to a rise in the equilibrium price of goods
   B   shifts the supply curve of a good leftwards
   C   leads to an increase in the equilibrium output of goods
   D   reduces the price elasticity of demand of goods

Answer on p. 118

Minimum prices

Minimum prices are price floors that establish a legal level below which prices are not allowed to fall. Examples of this intervention include the setting of a National Minimum Wage and guaranteed minimum prices paid to farmers for their agricultural products, such as with the European Union's Common Agricultural Policy (CAP).

> **Minimum price:** a price floor placed above the free market equilibrium price.

The impact of a minimum price is shown in Figure 5.7. A minimum price (P_1) set above the free market price (P^*) for a good will create excess supply, equal to $Q_S - Q_D$, as shown in the diagram.

Advantages of minimum prices

They give producers a guaranteed minimum price and income, which helps to generate a reasonable standard of living, such as in the case of farmers in less developed countries.

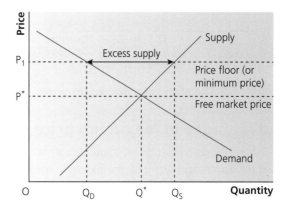

Figure 5.7 The effect of a minimum price

They encourage production of essential products, such as the foodstuffs produced by EU farmers covered by the CAP.

Excess supplies may be bought up and stored; to be released in times of future shortage.

Disadvantages of minimum prices

Consumers must pay a higher price, reducing their disposable income.

They can encourage over-production, especially in the case of the CAP, which is an inefficient use of resources. This excess supply may need to be put into storage, which generates further costs.

If governments or other authorities have to purchase excess supplies, this leads to opportunity costs, i.e. these funds could have been used elsewhere.

They may reduce international competitiveness if the price is raised above those of foreign competitors.

In the case of interventions to reduce the affordability of demerit goods, such as hard drugs or alcohol, they may encourage people to seek cheaper, potentially more harmful alternatives, leading to government failure.

Maximum prices

A **maximum price** is an upper limit, or price ceiling, above which prices are not permitted to rise. The justification for their use is usually that the free market equilibrium price would be too high for many consumers, leading to problems of reduced affordability. Examples include rent controls in densely populated cities, and limits on the ability of utility companies to raise their price above the rate of inflation.

> **Maximum price:** a price ceiling above which prices are not permitted to rise.

The impact of a maximum price is shown in Figure 5.8. A maximum price (P_1) set below the free market price (P^*) for a good will create excess demand, equal to $Q_2 - Q_1$, as shown in the diagram.

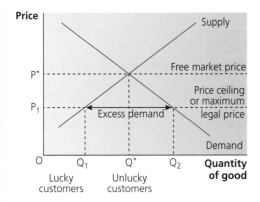

Figure 5.8 The effect of a maximum price

Advantages of maximum prices

Without a maximum price, some people would not be able to afford certain goods and services, for example some prescription medications. Thus maximum prices promote equity or fairness.

They can reduce the ability of firms with monopoly power to exploit consumers through charging higher prices.

Disadvantages of maximum prices

Some people who want a good or service will simply not be able to obtain it, leading to frustration and dissatisfaction.

The creation of excess demand implies queues, shortages and waiting lists, which, in the case of markets such as healthcare in the UK, can have serious implications.

Maximum prices may lead to the establishment of black markets for goods and services, such as secondary markets for music and sporting event tickets.

Exam tip

Practise drawing accurate minimum and maximum price diagrams and illustrate how they may lead to excess supply and excess demand respectively.

Typical mistake

Getting maximum price and minimum price the wrong way round. Remember that a maximum price is intended to stop prices rising too high and a minimum price is intended to stop prices falling too low. This distinction is often tested in multiple-choice questions.

Direct provision

REVISED

Sometimes a government might take the view that provision of a good or service cannot be left to the free market at all, since it may be provided in insufficient or excessive quantities (in the case of merit and demerit goods) or not at all (in the case of public goods). Typically, the government will organise provision of the product in question, then raise the necessary funds out of tax revenue. The government itself need not produce the good or service; it may pay a private sector firm to do this, wholly or partially. For example, it may pay a construction firm to build a new school.

Generally, these goods or services may be free or nearly free, 'at the point of consumption', so individuals do not have to worry about making a payment every time they attend state school or require medical treatment.

Regulation

REVISED

Regulations are rules or laws used to control or restrict the actions of economic agents in order to reduce market failure.

Examples of regulations used to tackle market failures include:
- banning smoking in public places
- a minimum legal age to drink alcohol

Regulation: rules or laws used to control or restrict the actions of economic agents in order to reduce market failure.

- maximum emissions levels on new cars
- noise thresholds on aeroplanes as they take off in urban areas
- establishing green-belt land around major cities
- setting up regulatory bodies (such as OFGEM) to restrict the activities of dominant firms

If firms or consumers do not adhere to the rules and laws they may be punished, for example with fines, limitations on trading activities, or even imprisonment.

Correcting information failure

Governments may attempt to intervene in markets where they believe that consumers consume either too many or too few goods or services because of a lack of information about the effects of consumption and production.

Goods which qualify as merit goods would be under-consumed in a free market because consumers lack knowledge, or are unable to make rational decisions, about the benefits of consumption, especially in the long run. Conversely, demerit goods would be over-consumed in a free market, again because of a lack of knowledge or ability to make rational choices about the problems arising from consumption.

Governments may use a range of methods to remedy information failure, all of which will affect the demand for the good or service in question, which, if done successfully, will bring the quantity demanded closer to the social optimum. Examples of attempts to correct information failure include:
- compulsory labelling on food, along with 'traffic-lighting' levels of fat, salt, etc.
- strong health warnings on packs of cigarettes
- TV advertising campaigns discouraging excessive alcohol consumption
- the publication of local and national league tables for schools and hospitals

There are several drawbacks of government attempts to correct information failure in these ways, however. For example, advertising campaigns often have a high cost and their effectiveness is questioned, particularly their ability in the long term to cause people to change their behaviour amidst the volume of information with which consumers are regularly bombarded. Indeed, the marketing power and skill of the world's leading soft drinks companies such as Coca-Cola may be greater than those of individual government attempts to counter them.

Government failure

Government failure is said to occur when government intervention in a market leads to a misallocation of resources. There are a number of reasons for government failure, and several causes may exist at the same time.

> **Government failure**: when government intervention in a market reduces overall economic welfare.

Reasons for government failure

Inadequate information

As noted earlier, governments often act with very imperfect information. For example, it is exteremely difficult in practice to place an accurate monetary value on external costs and benefits. For this reason, the subsequent indirect tax or subsidy used to deal with the issue is unlikely to internalise completely these externalities and lead to the social optimum, or allocatively efficient, quantity being produced and consumed.

Unintended consequences

A government seeking to reduce the consumption of demerit goods such as alcohol may impose a minimum price per unit of alcohol. However, this may lead to arguably more harmful intoxicants such as hard drugs becoming relatively cheap, encouraging greater consumption, with associated impacts upon health services and policing. Reduced consumption of alcohol may also lead to increased unemployment of people working in the drinks industry. These consequences may have been unforeseen by the government and so would be considered to be unintended.

Market distortions

Attempts by governments to correct market failure may lead to inefficiencies, surpluses and shortages. For example, a maximum price on aspects of healthcare such as prescriptions may lead to excess demand, while a minimum wage may lead to an excess supply of workers in some low-paid occupations.

Administrative costs

It is possible that the costs of researching and implementing any intervention may outweigh the benefit of the policy itself, leading to a worsening of the allocation of resources. For example, the cost of recruiting and paying a staff of inspectors to ensure firms and individuals adhere to specific regulations may exceed the size of the external cost arising from the market failure.

Regulatory capture

This is said to occur when the regulatory bodies (such as OFGEM in the case of gas and electricity suppliers) set up to oversee the behaviour of privatised monopolies come to be unduly influenced by the firms they have been set up to monitor. This is because, to an extent, the regulators depend upon the existence of dominant firms in such industries for their existence, and so may be more easily swayed.

Now test yourself

TESTED

10 Which one of the following is an example of government failure?
  A state provision of national defence
  B all subsidies given to firms
  C the government allowing the free market to raise the price of petrol
  D the government overproducing a merit good

Answer on p. 118

Exam practice

1 Market failure arises whenever firms:
   A   make workers redundant
   B   increase prices
   C   create negative externalities
   D   make a loss   [1]
2 The following table shows the marginal private and external benefits and the marginal private and
   external costs of a product provided by the free market.

Benefits/costs	£
Marginal private benefit	15
Marginal external benefit	12
Marginal private cost	15
Marginal external cost	0

   Government intervention in this market may improve economic welfare because the product is
   likely to be:
   A   an inferior good   B   a public good   C   a demerit good   D   a merit good   [1]
3 Market failure may be corrected if a government:
   A   provides public goods
   B   subsidises all private sector firms
   C   places an indirect tax on merit goods
   D   places a maximum price on demerit goods   [1]
4 Market failure may best be reduced by:
   A   the existence of merit goods
   B   reduced mobility of factors of production
   C   increasing economies of scale
   D   improving the availability of information to consumers   [1]
5 (a) Define the term 'demerit good'.   [3]
   (b) With the aid of a diagram, explain why individuals may consume too much unhealthy food.   [8]
6 Using a diagram, explain how a government subsidy may be used to correct the market failure
   associated with merit goods.   [8]
7 Evaluate the effectiveness of methods that could be used to tackle the under-consumption
   of merit goods such as education.   [25]

Answers and quick quizzes online

ONLINE

Summary

You should have an understanding of:
- The four key functions of prices.
- The meaning of market failure.
- The distinction between complete market failure and partial market failure.
- The key characteristics of a public good.
- The differences between a public good, a private good and a quasi-public good.
- The concept of an externality.
- Diagrams showing positive and negative externalities.
- How positive and negative externalities lead to market failure.

- The difference between a merit good and a demerit good.
- How the under-consumption of merit goods and over-consumption of demerit goods may lead to market failure.
- The concept of information failure.
- How monopoly may lead to market failure and a misallocation of resources.
- How income and wealth inequality may lead to market failure.
- How governments may intervene in markets in order to correct cases of market failure.
- Government failure: meaning and causes.

6 The measurement of macroeconomic performance

The objectives of government economic policy

Any government will aim to influence how the **macroeconomy** performs over time and will have **macroeconomic objectives**. These objectives are goals or aims that they wish to achieve. Macroeconomic objectives are the goals a government wants to achieve for the whole economy.

The tools and methods that are used to influence the macroeconomy are referred to as **economic policies**. Therefore the objectives of government economic policy are the goals a government would like to achieve through the manipulation of the various tools it has available to use.

The main objectives of government macroeconomic policy are outlined below.

> **Macroeconomics**: macroeconomics refers to the economy as a whole, i.e. on a national scale.
>
> **Macroeconomic objective**: a goal a government would like to achieve for the macroeconomy.
>
> **Economic policy**: the economic tools and instruments available for a government to use to influence economic performance.

Economic growth
REVISED

Economic growth measures how much the value of output produced in an economy (known as national income) has grown over a period of time, usually over one year. It is calculated as the percentage change in national income over a period of time.

> **Economic growth**: the change in national income measured over a period of time.

Price stability
REVISED

This is concerned with how fast the average level of prices of a range of goods and services rises over a period of one year.

Minimising unemployment
REVISED

This involves minimising the numbers of those of working age who are looking for work but are unable to find a job.

Stable balance of payments on current account
REVISED

The **balance of payments** measures the difference between the value of goods and services sold abroad and the value of goods and services bought from abroad.

> **Balance of payments**: the record of financial transactions between the UK and the rest of the world.

Balancing the budget
REVISED

The government would like the value of government expenditure and the value of taxation to be the same as each other so that the **government's budget** is balanced.

> **Government's budget**: the budget refers to the value of government spending compared with the money earned by the government through taxation over a period of time.

Achieving an equitable distribution of income

Incomes are not shared out equally across households in the economy. Achieving an equitable **distribution of income** means the government would like to ensure that the gap between the richest and poorest does not become excessively wide.

> **Distribution of income**: how evenly incomes are shared between individuals and households across the economy.

Now test yourself

TESTED

1 If national income in one year was £800 billion and rose in the following year to £820 billion, what was the rate of economic growth over this time period?

Answer on p. 118

Typical mistake

The level of national income is important but most people are more interested in the change in the level of national income — i.e. its rate of growth. Be careful to make it clear which one you are talking about.

Conflicts in achieving these objectives

REVISED

Achieving different economic objectives simultaneously is difficult. This is because there is the possibility of conflict arising in attempts to achieve different objectives at the same time.

A **policy conflict** that has occurred frequently concerns the conflict between minimising unemployment and achieving price stability. Success in reducing the level of unemployment has often come at the expense of prices rising at a faster rate, and vice versa.

The conflicts that exist are often said to exist only in the short term. It is suggested that in the long term, it is possible to achieve all the objectives at the same time, with no policy conflict. Some would argue that there is no conflict even in the short term. This is open to debate.

Policy conflict: attempts to achieve one economic objective move us further away from another economic objective.

Typical mistake

Do not assume that being unable to achieve an objective means it is not worth trying to achieve it. Getting as close as possible may be seen as good enough. Economics is about making the best use of scarce resources or getting as close as possible to the best use.

Exam tip

The concept of a trade-off in achieving multiple objectives is a good way of developing extended answers — and a way of evaluating the success of a policy.

Importance of economic objectives

REVISED

The following are generally seen as the main priorities among the government's economic objectives:
● economic growth
● price stability
● minimising unemployment

Governments do not view all their economic objectives as equally important. They have priorities in terms of which are considered more important to achieve. These priorities will change as circumstances change.

For example, after winning the 2015 general election, George Osborne, the Chancellor of the Exchequer, decided to make eliminating the budget deficit less of a priority than it had been in the previous parliament.

Exam tip

The conflict between objectives in the short term may not exist in the long term.

Similarly, some objectives have become less important over time. For example, achieving a stable balance of payments on current account is no longer seen as important as it was up until the 1970s.

Macroeconomic indicators

In order to assess how close we are to achieving economic objectives we have to examine the data from a range of macroeconomic indicators. These indicators each focus on an economic variable that measures economic performance. The main economic indicators are outlined below.

Real gross domestic product (GDP)

REVISED

Gross domestic product (GDP) is a measure of the **national income** of an economy. It is based on the value of all incomes earned in an economy over a period of time (data are produced every quarter, though the yearly figure is the one that attracts most attention).

Real GDP measures the value of GDP after removing the effect of price changes from its value. This ensures that an increase in GDP from one year to the next represents increased output of goods and services rather than just increases in prices.

Although there is no actual target for growth in real GDP, the government would like to achieve a positive rate — usually growth of between 2% and 3% per year.

> **Gross domestic product**: the term used widely to represent the national income of an economy.
>
> **National income**: the total income generated within an economy over a period of time.

Now test yourself

TESTED

2 If economic growth in 2015 was 2% but then fell in 2016 to 1%, what has happened to the level of GDP?

Answer on p. 118

Real GDP per capita

REVISED

Real GDP is often used to make comparisons between countries in terms of the standard of living enjoyed by the population.

To make comparisons more meaningful, average income per person is often used. This is known as real GDP **per capita** and it is calculated as follows:

$$\text{Real GDP per capita (measured in monetary units, e.g. £s)} = \frac{\text{real GDP (total) (£)}}{\text{population level}}$$

> **Real gross domestic product**: real variables are those adjusted for changes in the level of prices, adjusting real GDP national income for changes in average prices.
>
> **Per capita**: a variable adjusted to give an average amount per person.

Now test yourself

3 Calculate the GDP per capita of the UK and Norway based on the following estimates:

	GDP 2014 (US$ billions)	Population (estimate) (millions)
UK	2945	64
Norway	500	5.2

4 Explain why a government wants to achieve economic growth as one of its objectives.

Answers on p. 118

Exam tip

Real GDP per capita is very useful in telling us about the standard of living in a country but it doesn't take into account how that income is shared out — this depends on the distribution of income.

Typical mistake

When dealing with large numbers ensure you don't confuse millions and billions — always check to see if your answer makes sense.

Consumer price index (CPI) and retail price index (RPI)

One government objective is to achieve price stability. This is where the average level of prices is reasonably stable. An increase in the **price level** over time is referred to as **inflation**.

High and unstable inflation is something governments wish to avoid. As a result the government has a target **rate of inflation** that it wishes to achieve of 2%. This means that the government wishes to see the average level of prices rising by no more than 2% annually (actually the target allows a margin of error of 1%, which means inflation can still be on target as long as it is no lower than 1% and no higher than 3%).

In the UK, two main measures of the price level are used to record the rate of inflation:
● consumer price index (CPI)
● retail price index (RPI)

Both measures include the prices of goods and services typically bought by households in the UK.

Although the CPI measure is the 'official' measure used to calculate inflation, the RPI is still used by the government. For example, the prices of tickets set by rail companies are regulated by the government and can rise no faster than the inflation rate based on the RPI.

It is the job of the Bank of England (the UK's central bank) to achieve this inflation target.

Price level: the average level of prices of a range of goods and services at a point in time (measured monthly).

Inflation: an increase in the average level of prices measured over a period of time.

Inflation rate: the percentage change in the price level measured over the period of 1 year.

Typical mistake

Falling inflation does not mean falling prices — just that the rate of price increases is lower.

Now test yourself

5 If the rate of inflation falls from 3% to 2%, explain what is happening to average prices in this economy.

Answer on p. 118

Measures of unemployment

There are plenty of people who are not working in the economy (children, the elderly, those raising families), but people only count as part of the **unemployment** statistics if they are part of the **labour force** (i.e. those in work or actively seeking work).

In the UK there are two main measures of unemployment:

- **The claimant count** — includes the number of people receiving welfare benefits for being unemployed. The usual benefit received by those unemployed is jobseeker's allowance (JSA).
- **The Labour Force Survey (LFS)** — based on a monthly sample of people, it records those who report they are looking work but cannot find it, regardless of whether they receive benefits or not. This information is used to produce an estimate of the national unemployment level.

In the UK, the LFS measure is normally higher than the claimant count measure as it includes all those receiving benefits as well as those who do not qualify for (or do not wish to claim) benefits.

Although the level of unemployment (expressed as a number) is published, it is the rate of unemployment which will often be seen as more significant. The **unemployment rate** is calculated as:

$$\text{Unemployment rate (\%)} = \frac{\text{number of people unemployed}}{\text{size of labour force}} \times 100$$

Unemployment: those of working age who are currently out of work but are actively seeking work.

Labour force: those of working age who are either in work or actively seeking work.

Claimant count: the measure of unemployment in the UK that counts those who are receiving unemployment benefits.

Unemployment rate: the number of unemployed people expressed as a percentage of the current labour force.

Now test yourself

TESTED

6 Explain why the claimant count rate may be lower than the LFS measure of unemployment.

Answer on p. 118

Typical mistake

Many people lose or choose to leave their jobs, but the vast majority find work almost immediately.

Productivity

Productivity measures how much output is being produced by each unit of labour (such as per worker, or per hour worked). **Labour productivity** measures the output of workers, whereas **capital productivity** looks at the efficiency of machinery and equipment.

Economic growth in the long run mainly comes from improvements in productivity (i.e. getting more output from existing resources).

Improvements in productivity will come from making workers more efficient (either faster or better) in producing output and also improving the efficiency of the economy's capital equipment (machines etc.)

Productivity: a measure of efficiency comparing the level of output with the level of inputs.

Labour productivity: the output of the workforce compared with the amount of labour (either in people or in hours) used to produce the output.

Capital productivity: the output per item of capital equipment measured over a period of time.

Now test yourself

TESTED

7 Explain two reasons why labour productivity may not grow as fast as the government wishes.

Answer on p. 118

Exam tip

Be careful to distinguish between short-run and long-run growth when writing about economic growth.

Current account on the balance of payments

The balance of payments is divided into three sections: the **current account**, the capital account and the financial account. However, at AS level we are concerned only with the current account.

The main section of the current account relates to foreign trade, i.e.:
- exports of goods and services (produced in the UK but sold to foreigners)
- imports of goods and services (produced overseas but purchased by the UK)

The difference between these two values (exports minus imports) is referred to as the **balance of trade**.

   Value of exports > value of imports = trade surplus

   Value of exports < value of imports = trade deficit

Although the current account includes other components (which are explored in Chapter 8, see pages 96–97), it is foreign trade which largely determines the current account balance.

The UK normally has a surplus on the balance of trade for services but a deficit on the balance of trade for goods.

Overall, the UK normally experiences a **current account deficit**. The government would like to see this balance move closer towards a current account surplus.

> **Current account**: part of the balance of payments which looks at the net income flows earned through either trade in goods and services or the reward from investments located overseas.
>
> **Current account deficit**: where the flows of money from trade and other incomes out of the country are greater than the equivalent flows into the country.

> **Typical mistake**
>
> Many people — including many TV broadcasters — will talk about the balance of payments when they mean the current account of the balance of payments.

> **Exam tip**
>
> The balance of payments should always balance; it is the individual components of the balance of payments that may be in surplus or deficit.

Uses of index numbers

Index numbers are frequently used to illustrate economic variables when data are presented.

Index numbers are useful when making comparisons over periods of time. They are particularly useful when it is the size of changes in variables that need to be highlighted (rather than the actual values of the variables themselves).

Index numbers will start off with a value of 100 and this value is known as the **base year** value. The change in the index number will show how far the variable has moved away from its starting value.

For example, an index number of 120 would indicate that the variable's value had increased by 20% since the base year starting value. Presenting these index numbers as a line graph increases the ease with which the changes in values can be understood and interpreted.

> **Index number**: a number designed to be used to show the size of changes in a variable over time.

> **Exam tip**
>
> If two variables are translated into index numbers, even if they both start at 100, this does not mean they have the same value in reality — the index number is used to make comparisons and contrasts as the variables change.

UK production indices

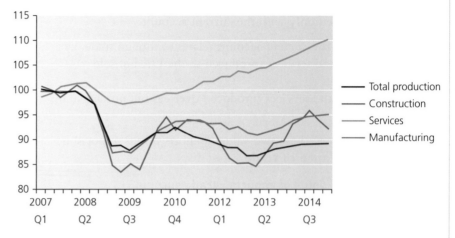

Figure 6.1 **Level of output in the production, manufacturing, construction and services industries (base year: 2007 = 100)**

Source: Office for National Statistics

This diagram shows the index of output for each of the main contributors to GDP: construction, services and manufacturing, along with total production.

We don't know the actual output level of each of these sectors but by using these as index numbers we can quickly see how each sector has performed in relation to the others. Key points would include:

- the output of all sectors fell in the recession of 2008–9
- recovery in all sectors started in 2009
- the services sector has grown quickly compared to other sectors

Although all sectors start with an index of 100, this does not mean their output was all at the same level — it is how the levels change over time that concerns us.

Now test yourself

TESTED

8 Explain why index numbers may be used to show changes in the price of a commodity over time.

Answer on p. 118

Consumer price index (CPI)

Controlling inflation is a major macroeconomic objective. In the UK, the inflation rate is measured through the annual percentage change in the CPI — an index number measuring the average level of prices for the UK.

The CPI is calculated by combining price data for the UK as a whole for a variety of different products bought by an imaginary 'typical' family. This means the CPI is meant to represent the spending patterns of a typical, average UK household.

The range of goods and services included in the calculation is often referred to as a **basket of goods and services**. This inflation 'basket' includes over 700 items and the prices of these are checked in thousands of shops across the UK each month.

The basket of goods and services is updated annually as new products emerge and old ones decline in popularity. For example, in 2015, E-cigarettes were added to this inflation 'basket' whereas frozen pizza was removed (we still like eating pizza, but largely prefer chilled ones!).

The CPI is a **weighted price index**. 'Weights' are attached to items in the CPI according to their relative importance to an average family in their spending patterns. For example, a doubling of the price of light bulbs will

Price index: an average level of prices based on a selection of goods bought by the typical household.

Basket of goods and services: the selection of products to be included within the price index based on typical household purchases.

Weighted price index: an average level of prices adjusted so that price changes in popular items affect the price index more than price changes in seldom-bought items.

have less impact on the CPI number than a doubling of the price of cars, or holidays, or restaurant meals because light bulbs are a less significant item in our average spending plans.

Issues with the CPI

As it is based on an 'imaginary' typical family, the CPI never really reflects anyone's exact spending patterns — how representative it is depends on how close an individual's spending patterns are to those on which the CPI is based.

The inflation 'basket' has to include many goods and services that not everyone buys; for example, most people don't smoke but cigarettes are still included within the basket to account for those who do.

Regular updates to the basket mean we are not always comparing like with like (i.e. the 2016 basket will differ from the 2015 basket), though the updated items are small in number.

No account is taken of the quality of the items included. A computer may cost slightly more in 2016 than in 2009 but it will be much better in terms of capability — does this mean it really has become more 'expensive'?

Typical mistake

House prices and mortgages are not in the CPI basket, so rapid house price increases or cuts in mortgage repayments will not show up in the CPI.

Exam tip

An inflation rate of zero means that on average prices are stable. In reality, even with a zero rate, some prices are rising and some are falling at the same time.

Revision activity

Make an A4 sheet with brief details on how each of the government's main objectives is measured in the UK.

Now test yourself

TESTED ☐

9 Give two reasons why inflation may not be a reliable indicator of price changes.
10 This table shows the weights used (expressed as percentages) within the CPI basket of goods and service used to calculate the UK inflation rate.

CPI (consumer price index)	Weight 2015 (%)	Weight 2014 (%)
Food and non-alcoholic beverages	11.0	11.2
Alcoholic beverages and tobacco	4.3	4.5
Clothing and footwear	7.0	7.2
Housing, water, electricity, gas and other fuels	12.8	12.9
Furniture, household equipment and maintenance	5.9	6.0
Health	2.5	2.4
Transport	14.9	15.2
Communication	3.1	3.2
Recreation and culture	14.7	14.4
Education	2.6	2.2
Restaurants and hotels	12.1	12.0
Miscellaneous goods and services	9.1	8.8

Source: Office for National Statistics

(a) Explain why the largest weightings are attached to housing, transport, and recreation and culture.
(b) Explain why you think the weights used in the CPI are updated and, if necessary, changed each year.

Answers on p. 118

6 The measurement of macroeconomic performance

Exam practice

	GDP ($) 2013 estimates	Population (millions) 2013
USA	16720	304
China	13390	1330
India	4990	1150
Germany	3227	82

Source: CIA World Factbook

1 Based on the data above:
   (a) Calculate the GDP per capita for 2013 for each country.   [4]
   (b) Which of the countries has the (i) largest and (ii) lowest GDP per capita?   [2]
   (c) Explain two limitations of using GDP per capita when making judgements about living
       standards in different countries.   [8]

Answers and quick quizzes online

ONLINE

Summary

You should have an understanding of:
- What the government's main economic objectives are and how these are measured through indicators in the UK.
- How there may be policy conflicts in attempting to achieve multiple objectives.
- How index numbers are used to show changes in economic variables.
- What is meant by a price index and how this is used in the UK.

The circular flow of income

National income

We know that national income refers to the income of an economy (a country) earned by all workers and businesses over a period of time. Income is a flow variable that is measured over time. A stock variable, such as household wealth, is measured at a point in time.

National income can be calculated in three ways:
1 expenditure method
2 income method
3 output method

Expenditure method

This involves adding up all the spending over a period of time:
- **Consumption** (C)
- **Investment** (I)
- **Government expenditure** (G) (not including welfare benefits paid out)
- **Net exports** $(X - M)$

Income method

This involves adding up all incomes earned over a period of time:
- wages and salaries earned by those in work
- rent earned by those who allow their land and property to be used by others
- interest earned by those who invest capital in financial assets
- profits earned by companies trading goods and services

Output method

This involves totalling the value of all output produced in the economy for a period of time for each sector of the economy. Steps need to be taken to avoid double counting; for example, the output of the steel industry may be used in the production of cars and this should appear only once.

For the non-traded sectors, such as state education and the NHS, a value of their output is based on the cost of their provision, i.e. how much the government spends on these sectors over a period of time.

Comparison of the three methods

All three methods should give the same value as they include all the same economics transactions for a period of time, but each method views the transaction from a different perspective, i.e. one person's spending is another person's income. In reality, the totals for the three methods will often differ by a small amount, which is mainly due to mistakes and unrecorded transactions.

Bear in mind that:

national income = national expenditure = national output

> **Consumption**: spending by households on goods and services.
>
> **Investment**: spending by businesses on additions to the capital stock, such as new premises or equipment, or the building up of inventory (stock) levels.
>
> **Government expenditure**: spending by the government at both national and local levels within the economy.
>
> **Net exports**: the value of exports less the value of imports in an economy over a period of time.

> **Exam tip**
>
> Although you will not be directly tested on the construction of the national income accounts, it is useful to see the three methods and how they are related.

Now test yourself

1 Explain why total expenditure in an economy should equal total income.

Answer on p. 118

Real national income versus nominal national income

Real national income measures national income after removing the effect of price changes from its value. This means that any increase in real income refers to increases in output (or income) and does not merely represent higher prices charged for the same amount of production.

National income that is unadjusted for changes in prices is known as **nominal national income** or money national income.

Nominal national income: national income unadjusted for changes in prices (also known as money income).

How to calculate real national income is shown in the following example.

Example

If nominal national income rose from £1300 billion in 2015 to £1400 billion in 2016, then the nominal increase of £100 billion would represent a percentage increase of 7.7% between 2015 and 2016. However, if we are told that the price index rose from 100 to 104 over this period then part of the rise in national income is explained by price increases rather than increases in output.

Real national income (NI) would be calculated as follows:

$$\text{Real NI} = \text{nominal NI} \times \left(\frac{\text{price level in previous year}}{\text{price level in current year}}\right)$$

Real GDP for 2016 is calculated as follows:

$$\text{Real NI} = \pounds1400\,\text{bn} \times \left(\frac{100}{104}\right) = \pounds1346.15\,\text{bn}$$

Economic growth would be measured by the percentage change in real national income over the period of one year. For example, using the data from the previous question, economic growth could be calculated as follows:

$$\text{Economic growth for 2016} = \left(\frac{\pounds1346.15\,\text{bn} - \pounds1300\,\text{bn}}{\pounds1300\,\text{bn}}\right) \times 100 = 3.6\%$$

Now test yourself

2 From the data here, calculate:
  (a) real GDP for 2016
  (b) economic growth for 2016 (in real terms)

Year	Nominal GDP (€) (billions)	Price level
2015	800	150
2016	980	175

Answer on p. 118

GDP and real national income

REVISED

Real national income is one of the most used macroeconomic variables. It is often referred to as gross domestic product (GDP). Technically, real national income and real GDP are not the same variable as some UK national income comes from incomes earned outside the UK but still belonging to UK citizens.

Gross national income (real GNI) includes incomes from overseas assets. However, the difference between GDP and GNI is small and these terms are often used interchangeably.

Uses of real national income

REVISED

Real national income provides useful information:
● It is a measure of how successful the economy is — countries are often ranked in importance by the size of their national incomes.
● It shows how well off the population is — through measuring national income per person.
● It allows a government to estimate how much can be collected in taxation (most taxes are placed on incomes and expenditure — both measures of national income).

Now test yourself

TESTED

3 State three ways in which real national income per capita does not provide a good indicator of living standards within a country.

Answer on p. 118

The circular flow of income model

REVISED

A simple circular flow of income

The connection between national income, output and expenditure can be incorporated into a simple model of the macroeconomy known as the **circular flow of income**. This shows how money flows around the economy as a result of the transactions taking place.

> **Circular flow of income**: a model of the economy where income and spending flow between households and firms.

In a simple two-sector economy (consisting of just the business and the household sector), businesses employ factors of production supplied by households to produce goods and services.

In return, as Figure 7.1 shows, households supply their labour (and other factors) and earn incomes from firms, which households then spend as consumption on goods and services.

The level of national income will remain constant as money flows from households to businesses and back again; although obviously this is not how the actual UK economy behaves.

> **Injections**: extra money placed into the circular flow of income.
>
> **Withdrawals**: money taken out of the circular flow of income.

A modified model of the circular flow allows for **injections** (in the form of investment by businesses) and **withdrawals** (in the form of household savings).

If injections are greater than withdrawals, more is being added to the circular flow and income overall will rise. The opposite is also true; a greater quantity of withdrawals than injections will lead to falling income.

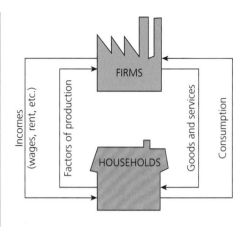

Figure 7.1 **The circular flow of income**

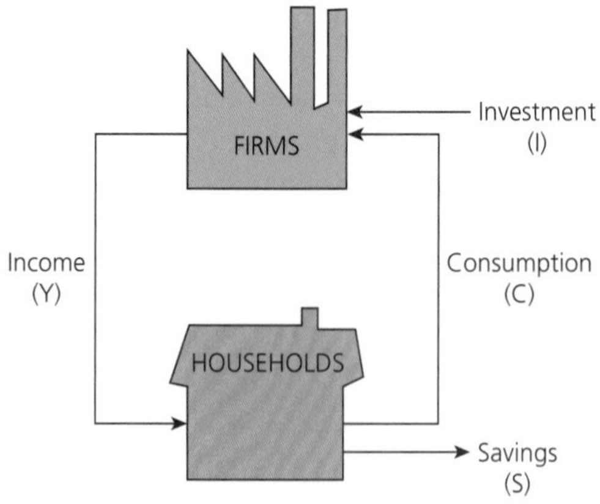

Figure 7.2 **The two-sector model of the circular flow of income, with money withdrawn in the form of savings and injected back into the flow in the form of investment**

A more complex circular flow of income

Adding the government sector and the foreign sector to the model gives the following representation of the circular flow of income.

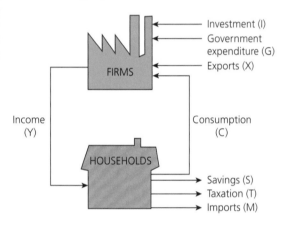

Figure 7.3 **The circular flow of income with the addition of the government sector and foreign trade sector**

There are now three injections into the circular flow:
- investment (I)
- government expenditure (G)
- exports (X)

There are now also three withdrawals from the circular flow:
- savings (S)
- taxation (T)
- imports (M)

Equilibrium in the circular flow of income

Macroeconomic equilibrium is reached in the circular flow of income model if there is no pressure on national income to rise or to fall.

In the circular flow model the economy will remain in equilibrium as long as the total of planned injections is equal to the total of planned withdrawals. This can be stated as:

$$I + G + X = S + T + M$$

If the total injections are higher than total withdrawals, then national income will increase until a new equilibrium level of national income

> **Macroeconomic equilibrium**: the level of national income where there is no tendency for the level to change.

is reached when injections are again equal to withdrawals. Likewise, if withdrawals are greater than injections, then national income will fall until a new equilibrium is reached at a lower level of national income.

To summarise:
- injections = withdrawals: macroeconomic equilibrium
- injections > withdrawals: national income increases
- withdrawals < injections: national income falls

If a government wishes to increase national income in the economy then it could increase government spending. As long as nothing else changes, this should lead to an increase in the level of national income.

Now test yourself

TESTED ☐

4 Using the table of data here, state whether the economy is in equilibrium. Back this up with numerical justification. Explain what is likely to happen to national income.

	£ billion
Investment	120
Exports	80
Imports	140
Government expenditure	600
Taxation	550
Savings	75

Answer on p. 118

Aggregate demand and aggregate supply

Aggregate demand

REVISED ☐

Another model for looking at macroeconomic equilibrium is **aggregate demand** (AD) and aggregate supply (AS) analysis.

This considers the equilibrium position of the macroeconomy in terms of the level of real national income (or real GDP) and also the price level at that equilibrium position.

It is more useful than the circular flow of income model as it is possible to see the potential inflationary and deflationary impacts of changes in government policy, as well as the effect on national income.

Aggregate demand consists of:
- consumption (C)
- investment (I)
- government expenditure (G)
- net exports (exports − imports) (X − M)

$$AD = C + I + G + X - M$$

Aggregate demand: total planned spending in an economy over a period of time at any given price level. It is calculated as $C + I + G + X - M$.

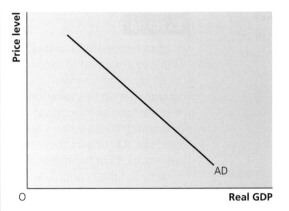

Figure 7.4 Aggregate demand (AD) showing the amounts of planned expenditure that would occur at different price levels

The AD curve appears as downward sloping from left to right. This is because:

- At a lower price level, the value of any assets such as property and shares will increase in real terms. This may lead to a **wealth effect** — making consumers feel as though they have greater **wealth**, leading to higher consumption levels.
- A lower price level will make UK exports more price competitive (compared to foreign substitutes), thus leading to a higher level of exports sold abroad. It will also make domestic goods relatively cheaper than imported goods, which should reduce the level of imports.

Typical mistake

Label the axes correctly — it is price level and real GDP (or real output, or real national income) on the axes. Do not use price (P) and quantity (Q); they belong to microeconomics.

Wealth effect: increases in the value of a household's assets cause people to feel wealthier and encourage them to spend more of their current income (or to borrow more to finance the increases in spending).

Wealth: wealth refers to the value of the assets held by households. Most wealth will be held in the value of property (or equity) owned by the household.

Factors determining aggregate demand

REVISED

Higher levels of national income will mean there is more money to spend. However, even with a constant level of national income there will be changes to the level of aggregate demand if one of its components changes.

Consumption

Consumption is the largest competent of aggregate demand, comprising around 70% of overall AD. Households do not spend all of their income on consumption, as they will make decisions on whether or not to save. Factors affecting consumption include the following.

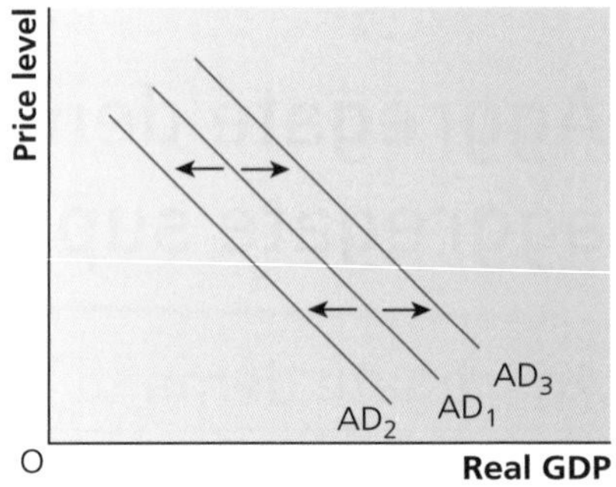

Figure 7.5 Shifts in the AD curve

Interest rates

Interest rates affect consumption in three ways:

- If interest rates rise then those who have variable-rate mortgages will find that their monthly payments increase, which means less money is available for households to spend on consumption.
- Higher interest rates reduce the desirability of households to engage in credit-financed consumption (i.e. consumption financed by borrowing).
- Higher interest rates increase the reward for savings which, by definition, reduces the level of consumption.

Interest rate: the cost of borrowing money expressed as a percentage of the amount borrowed.

Exam tip

Although interest rates affect consumption in three ways, the incentive to save 'effect' is not significant.

Consumer confidence

Households will have varying degrees of confidence about the future. If they feel that their incomes are likely to fall or that their jobs are less secure, they are more likely to reduce their current consumption in preparation for these times. The converse is also true. Therefore, consumption will rise and fall in line with consumer confidence.

Taxation

Changes in taxation will affect how much households have to spend. Increases in taxes, especially income taxes, will reduce the disposable income of households, leading to reduced overall consumption.

Wealth

If household wealth increases then this will have a positive 'wealth effect' on households, which means they will probably spend more on consumer goods and services (even if financed by borrowing).

Unemployment

If more people are unemployed and relying on welfare benefits, then the level of consumption is likely to be lower.

Investment

The main determinants of investment are described below.

Interest rates

Increases in interest rates raise the cost of borrowing and will reduce the profitability of any investment project. Even if investment is not financed by borrowing, higher interest rates will raise the opportunity cost of using money for investment purposes.

Business confidence

If businesses expect that sales will increase in the future then they will be more likely to spend money on investment goods, so as to increase their productive capacity to satisfy increased future demand for their goods and services.

Tax

Companies are taxed on their profits (in the UK this is called corporation tax) and if this tax is lowered, businesses will have more of their profits available to spend. This is likely to lead to higher investment.

Technology

New technologies should increase efficiency of production, which should lead to firms investing more in new technology in order to increase their profitability.

Introduction of new technologies will generate new markets for firms and will lead to firms investing more as a way of exploiting the new opportunities that technology brings.

Accelerator theory

The **accelerator theory** of investment states that increases and decreases in the rate of growth of national income will lead to even larger increases in the level of investment.

> **Accelerator theory**: where increases in national income lead to firms spending more on investment, in order to expand their capacity to exploit the rising income.

If growth in national income increases, then firms will need a larger productive capacity in order to produce a higher level of output to meet the higher level of spending in the economy.

Similarly, if the growth rate of national income falls then firms will not need as a large a productive capacity and therefore investment in maintaining capacity can fall.

> **Capital stock**: the value of the existing level of investment products in an economy at a point in time (i.e. the value of machinery, equipment, premises, etc.)

Typical mistake

Investment should not be confused with savings. The two are often used interchangeably in everyday usage but in economics they are distinct. In economics, 'savings' refers to household income that is not spent on consumer products. 'Investment' refers to spending by businesses on additions to overall **capital stock**.

Government expenditure

Governments will spend money on a number of areas within the economy, including:

- **public services** — such as health, education, transport and defence
- **local government services** — such as libraries and other council services
- **welfare expenditure** — pensions, care allowances, tax credits and benefits
- **interest on debt** — payments on outstanding government debt accumulated over time

Government expenditure is financed through taxation. However, it is very likely that the two totals of government spending and tax revenue collected will not be equal. The difference is known as the **budget balance**. It is highly likely that the budget will be in **deficit** (or less likely, in **surplus** or **balanced**).

> **Budget balance**: the difference between government spending and the taxation revenue collected.
>
> **Budget deficit**: government expenditure > taxation.
>
> **Budget surplus**: government expenditure < taxation.
>
> **Balanced budget**: government expenditure = taxation.

Net exports (exports – imports)

Exports and imports are affected by the following:

- **exchange rates**
- foreign growth
- UK growth
- relative inflation

> **Exchange rate**: the price of one currency expressed in terms of another currency.

All these factors are explored in Chapter 8 (see pages 97–98). It might be worth reading ahead if you need a reminder.

Now test yourself

TESTED ☐

5 Draw an aggregate demand curve and show any shifts in the curve that may result from each of the following:
  (a) an increase in house prices boosting consumer confidence
  (b) a rise in interest rates
  (c) an increase in tuition fees
  (d) a rise in inflation rates amongst EU states

Answer on p. 119

Revision activity

Make a mind map showing all the factors that will affect the level of consumption in an economy.

The multiplier process

Any change in a component of AD will shift the AD curve. Changes in AD will also be affected by the **multiplier process**.

This multiplier effect occurs because any extra spending creates income for another person or business. This extra income will in turn be spent again, thus creating income elsewhere for another group, and so on.

The further increases in income will not continue for ever and will decrease in size as extra income is taxed, saved or spent on imports, meaning less is 'passed on' in the circular flow with each extra transaction.

The size of the multiplier process can be determined by comparing the size of the overall change in national income with the size of the initial change in aggregate demand.

> **Multiplier process**: how a change in aggregate demand leads to a proportionately larger change in overall national income.

Example

A government decides to spend an extra £400 million on a new bypass. It is estimated that national income, as a result, eventually rose by £1000 million. What was the size of the multiplier?

$$\text{Size of the multiplier} = \frac{\text{change in national income}}{\text{initial change in AD}} = \frac{£1000m}{£400m} = 2.5$$

Negative multiplier

Although the multiplier process might sound a very useful way for a government to boost national income with a smaller increase in government spending, the multiplier can also work in the opposite direction. A fall in any of the components of aggregate demand will lead to a proportionately larger fall in overall national income. This effect is sometimes referred to as the 'negative' or 'backwards' multiplier effect.

> **Exam tip**
>
> In reality, the size of the multiplier is likely to be quite small; not much bigger than 1.

Now test yourself

6 Explain why an initial rise in aggregate demand does not lead to continual rises in national income as spending and incomes are passed on around the economy.

Answer on p. 119

Aggregate supply

The level of **aggregate supply** is based on the various costs incurred by a firm when producing output. We distinguish between **short-run aggregate supply** (SRAS) and **long-run aggregate supply** (LRAS).

> **Aggregate supply**: the total quantity of output that all the firms in the economy are willing to produce at a given price level.
>
> **Short-run aggregate supply**: how much firms will produce at a given price level in the short term.
>
> **Long-run aggregate supply**: how much firms will produce in the long run. This will be where an economy is producing its maximum potential output level and will be independent of the price level.

Determinants of short-run aggregate supply (SRAS)

The short-run refers to the period of time during which the prices of factors of production are constant.

In the short run, the aggregate supply curve slopes upwards — there is a positive relationship between the price level and the quantity of output firms are willing to produce and supply.

If any of the production costs change due to changes in the external environment, then the SRAS curve will shift. These changes would include:

- **Money wage rates** — if wage rates paid to workers increase, then firms will be less willing to supply output as it is less profitable to do so. Therefore there will be a leftward shift in the SRAS.
- **Changes in the cost of raw materials** — if the cost of materials increases, this will reduce the profitability of production, leading to firms being less willing to supply output. Higher costs will shift the SRAS to the left.
- **Business taxation** — businesses will incur certain taxes as part of their operations. Changes in indirect taxes, such as value added tax (VAT), will influence the profitability of production. Higher indirect taxes will lead to a leftward shift in SRAS as firms reduce the amount they are willing to produce.
- **Productivity** — if productivity increases, then firms will find it more profitable to supply greater quantities of output and therefore the SRAS curve will shift to the right.
- **Exchange rate changes** — a change in the exchange rate will alter the price a business pays for imported materials. A fall in the exchange rate will mean imports are more expensive and this will increase production costs for firms that import, shifting the SRAS leftward.

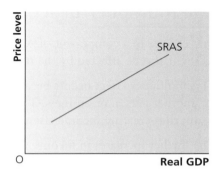

Figure 7.6 The SRAS curve, showing that as the price level increases, firms will be willing to supply more

> **Typical mistake**
>
> Be careful: a rise in the price level moves us along the SRAS curve — it does not shift the curve.

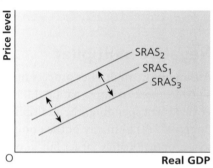

Figure 7.7 Shifts in the SRAS curve

Now test yourself

TESTED ☐

7 Draw a short-run aggregate supply (SRAS) curve and show shifts in the curve based on the following changes:
   (a) a fall in the price of imports
   (b) workers becoming more efficient in production
   (c) the oil price falling
   (d) a higher rate of VAT introduced

Answer on p. 119

> **Exam tip**
>
> The gradient of the SRAS is open to debate. Many economists believe that the SRAS in reality is not a straight, upward-sloping line but rather a curve which starts off with a fairly shallow gradient and then sharply curves upwards, becoming almost vertical the closer the economy gets to capacity. However, all the variants of the AS curve that appear here can be used in the exam.

Figure 7.8 gives an alternative approach to the SRAS curve. This version is useful for showing how increases in AD can be increasingly inflationary, the closer the economy's maximum output level (shown as Max) becomes.

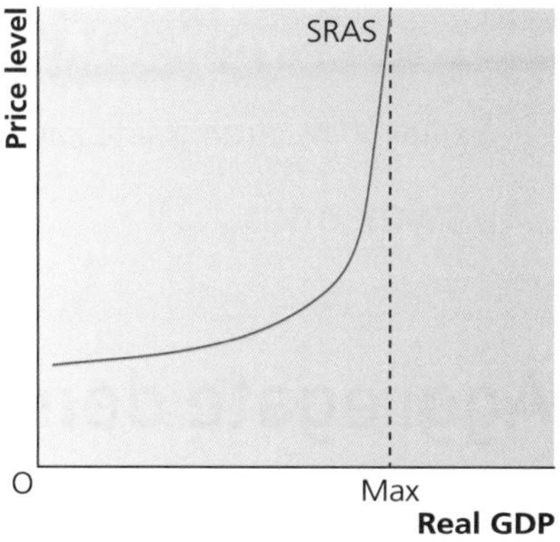

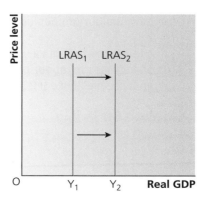

Figure 7.8 An alternative approach to the SRAS curve

Determinants of long-run aggregate supply (LRAS)

The long run is defined as the time period when the costs of the factors of production may vary. The LRAS curve is assumed to be vertical. This means that in the long run, the amount of output firms are willing to produce is unaffected by changes in the price level.

The LRAS represents the maximum amount an economy can produce — it represents the normal capacity output level for the economy and is determined by the following factors.

Technology

Advances in technology increase the amount firms can produce with the same resources available. This will therefore shift the LRAS curve to the right, increasing the capacity of the economy.

Productivity

As workers become more skilled, they are likely to become more productive, meaning that more can be produced in the same of amount of time (or with the same quantity of workers). This will increase the capacity level of an economy and therefore the LRAS curve shifts rightward with increases in productivity.

Factor mobility

How willing workers are to move around the country to fill job vacancies, and how able workers are to retrain themselves so they can take up job vacancies in other industries, will affect the LRAS. Increases in workers' willingness to swap locations and types of job will improve factor mobility, which means an economy can produce more output overall.

Enterprise

Encouraging more people to become entrepreneurs and set up their own businesses will increase the capacity of an economy and will shift the LRAS curve rightward. Governments therefore often adopt measures to make it easier for people to set up and run their own businesses.

Economic incentives and attitudes

Government policy can shift the position of the LRAS curve. For example, incentives in taxes and benefits, as well as changes in legislation, can affect how willing people are to work in the first place and how long, and how hard, they will work within their jobs. These economic incentives and how attitudes to work can be influenced are covered in the section on supply-side policies (see Chapter 9, pages 110–15).

Figure 7.9 shows LRAS as vertical. This implies that in the long run the economy will operate at its maximum potential level, and this can be increased only through factors affecting the long-run aggregate supply curve.

> **Exam tip**
>
> The time period for the short run and the long run is not fixed — economists disagree over how long these periods are.

Figure 7.9 Shifts in a vertical LRAS curve

8 Explain how cutting subsidies for childcare can lead to a leftward shift in the LRAS.

Answer on p. 119

Aggregate demand and aggregate supply analysis

Short-run macroeconomic equilibrium

REVISED

The interaction between AD and SRAS will give us the macroeconomic equilibrium position for an economy. Unless either AD or AS changes (i.e. shifts), this equilibrium position will be maintained.

Figure 7.10 shows that an increase in AD will lead to a movement along the SRAS curve, which gives both a higher real output level and a higher price level.

Figure 7.11 indicates that a decrease in SRAS (shown as a leftward shift in the SRAS curve) leads to movement along the AD curve, resulting in both lower real output level and a higher price level.

Typical mistake

Remember that shifts in one curve will cause movements along the other curve.

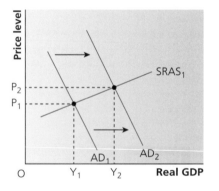

Figure 7.10 The effect of an increase in the AD curve

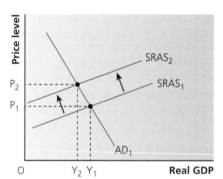

Figure 7.11 The effect of a decrease in SRAS

9 On this diagram, the equilibrium position is A. State which will be the new equilibrium positions when the following changes take place:
  (a) a fall in the cost of raw materials and a cut in income tax
  (b) an increase in labour productivity
  (c) an increase in exports

Answer on p. 119

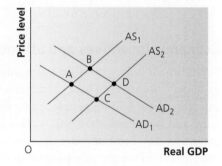

AD/AS analysis and government economic objectives

REVISED

The equilibrium position gives information about how the economy is performing. It shows the real level of national income and the price level. From this information, further assessments can be made about progress towards the government's economic objectives:

- **Economic growth:** This is measured as the change in real national income. It is possible to see if this objective is being achieved; for instance, falling output may indicate that a recession is occurring.
- **Employment:** Jobs depend partly on spending, so moving rightward on the horizontal axis (to a higher level of national income) will lead to a greater demand for workers, so output can increase in response to higher spending. Similarly, a fall in the level of national income is likely to lead to higher unemployment as fewer workers will be needed once output and spending levels have reduced.
- **Inflation:** Changes in the price level reveal whether the economy is experiencing inflation (in the case of a rise in the price level) or deflation (where the price level falls).

Remember, any change in AD is likely to have a greater overall effect on national income due to the multiplier process. This means that it may be difficult to position the AD curve exactly, given the uncertainty over the size of the multiplier.

Long-run macroeconomic equilibrium

REVISED

The long-run equilibrium position occurs where aggregate demand (AD) intersects with the long-run aggregate supply (LRAS) curve (see Figure 7.12). This always occurs at the maximum output level for an economy.

Given that the LRAS curve is vertical, this represents the normal capacity of real output in the economy. Increases in AD mean the equilibrium position moves upwards along the LRAS curve with no increase in real output. The only effect of higher AD in the long run is a higher price level, i.e. it has only inflationary consequences.

A rightward shift in the LRAS curve can be thought of as an outward shift of the production possibility curve (PPC), as it enables more output to be produced with the existing stock of resources. This is referred to as long-run growth.

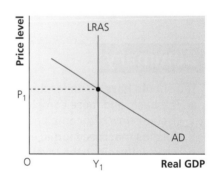

Figure 7.12 Long-run equilibrium

Typical mistake

Even if the economy is operating on the vertical section of the aggregate supply curve, do not assume this means zero unemployment. Operating at this position would mean no unemployment caused by lack of demand (see Chapter 8).

Revision activity

Produce a set of clear AD/AS diagrams for each type of movement and shift.

Now test yourself

TESTED

10 Using an AD/AS diagram, explain how investment in education may lead to a reduction in unemployment.

Answer on p. 119

Exam practice

A recently published report estimated that government support for the UK's screen industries adds more than £6 billion to the UK economy. This industry contains the UK's film, high-end TV, computer games and animation sectors and is seen as one of the UK's modern success stories. It is believed that each pound of support the government gives the industry actually benefits the whole UK economy significantly more. Spill-over benefits have been identified as including increased tourism and merchandising opportunities for UK toy manufacturers.

The UK film industry contributes nearly 40 000 jobs directly to the UK economy but also helps to generate jobs in other industries, such as the set-design, camera and lighting technology industries. It is estimated that another 60 000 jobs are indirectly created as a result of the continued success of the film industry.

A spokesperson for the industry stated that 'We welcome the financial support the British government gives the industry. As the report highlights, there are significant multiplier benefits for the UK as a whole from this help. The report estimates that the UK is £6 billion better off, which is commendable, especially when other sectors are struggling.'

1 Define the term 'multiplier'. [3]
2 It is estimated that the UK economy is £6 billion larger as a result of the government support described in the extract. If the government support totalled £1.5 billion, how big is the economic multiplier? [4]
3 Using an AD/AS diagram, analyse the effect of this government investment on the UK's economic performance. [8]
4 Explain three other policies a government could adopt to encourage further private sector investment into industries like the one mentioned in the extract. [10]

Answers and quick quizzes online

ONLINE

Summary

You should have an understanding of:
- The basic and more complex models of the circular flow of income and how an economy reaches macroeconomic equilibrium.
- What determines the level of aggregate demand, what factors would shift this curve and what would move us along the curve.

- The determinants of both the short-run and long-run aggregate supply curves and how changes in these factors will shift both curves.
- What is meant by macroeconomic equilibrium in the AD/AS model and how to show this diagrammatically.

8 Economic performance

Economic growth and the economic cycle

Short-run and long-run economic growth REVISED ☐

Short-run economic growth arises out of increased use of previously unemployed resources (workers or capital stock) resulting in increased overall output. This will appear as a movement from a point within an economy's production possibility curve (PPC) to a place either on or closer to the actual PPC boundary.

Long-run economic growth arises out of increases in long-run aggregate supply. This can be shown as either a rightward shift in the long-run aggregate supply (LRAS) curve or a shift outwards of the PPC.

As Figure 8.1 shows, short-run growth involves utilising previously unemployed factors within an economy (e.g. moving from point A to point B). Long-run growth involves expanding the capacity of the economy – shifting the PPC further out (point B to point C).

> **Short-run economic growth**: growth based on increased utilisation of unemployed resources.
>
> **Long-run economic growth**: growth based on increasing the potential output level of the economy.

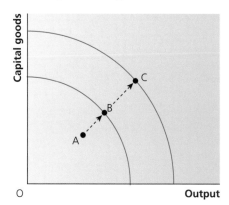

Figure 8.1 Short-run and long-run economic growth

Determinants of short-run growth

Short-run growth can be caused by an increase in either (or both) of the following:
- increases in aggregate demand (AD)
- increases in short-run aggregate supply (SRAS)

In most cases, it is increases in AD that provide the stimulus for short-run growth. An alternative name for short-run growth is **actual growth**. This is the type of growth that features more prominently in news stories and is measured by the percentage change in GDP.

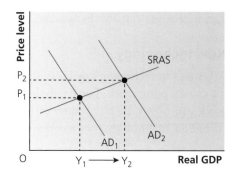

Figure 8.2 Increases in AD will produce short-run growth in the economy

Determinants of long-run growth

Long-run growth comes from increases in the productive capacity of the economy. These increases arise from improvements on the 'supply side' of the economy, which result from improvements in the quantity and quality of the factors of production available to an economy. Long-run growth is normally shown by a rightward shift of the LRAS curve, from $LRAS_1$ to $LRAS_2$ in Figure 8.3.

Factors which would increase long-run growth include those listed below.

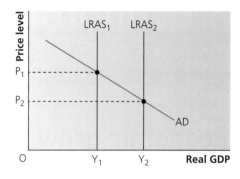

Figure 8.3 Shifts in the LRAS curve generate long-run growth

Increases in the labour force (labour supply)

Population size limits the labour supply but this can be increased through allowing more immigration into an economy.

Increasing the retirement age or encouraging people who are currently **economically inactive** to enter the workforce will also increase the labour supply.

Making it financially less attractive to remain out of work will increase the labour supply. This can be achieved either by paying less generous unemployment benefits, or by increasing incentives for the unemployed to take work (such as through cutting income tax paid, or allowing tax credits to those on low incomes).

> **Economically inactive:** those of working age who are not in work and not looking for work.

Improvements in labour productivity

An increase in the skills level of the workforce should lead to an increase in the amount that can be produced. Therefore increases in training undertaken by workers should boost long-run growth.

Capital investment

Investment contributes both to short-run growth (through increased AD) and to long-run growth (through increases to LRAS).

More investment in capital stock (premises, equipment, machinery, etc.) will enable businesses to produce more goods and services.

Governments can encourage businesses to invest by creating a more stable macroeconomic climate, which means they can plan investment with greater confidence.

Tax incentives can also be used to encourage investment.

New technology

Advances in technology will usually lead to productivity improvements for capital equipment. For example, much design and manufacturing work can now take place more efficiently through robotic and computer technology.

Technology improvements therefore raise the ability of an economy to produce more output with a given capital stock.

Education

Improvements to education within schools, colleges and universities should lead to improvements in worker productivity.

Occupational immobility can be reduced by ensuring education prepares a future workforce for a variety of occupations.

Government policy

There are a number of polices a government can use to encourage long-run growth. These are collectively referred to as 'supply-side' policies and are covered in Chapter 9 (pages 110–15).

Long-run growth is often referred to as **trend growth**. It is estimated to be somewhere between 2% to 2.5% a year in the UK.

Although the actual short-run rate of economic growth can rise beyond the long-run trend growth rate for short periods of time, it is long-run trend growth that represents the overall long-term limit to economic growth.

Attempts to encourage short-run growth in excess of long-run growth for a prolonged period of time are likely to lead to inflationary pressures.

Trend growth: the rate of growth in LRAS over time, representing the maximum potential capacity of the UK economy.

Exam tips

- An excellent contrasting point is that policies to promote long-run growth will take many years to be fully effective but will require large amounts of money to be spent in the short run (e.g. a high-speed railway).
- It is worth noting that some of the factors contributing to long-run growth will not arise from government policy and may just be the result of other factors, such as breakthroughs in technology.

Typical mistake

Although policies to prompt long-run growth may be desirable, do not forget that most will carry an opportunity cost in that they will cost money.

Now test yourself

TESTED

1 Which two of the following will lead to an increase in LRAS?
   A higher exports
   B reduced imports
   C advances in technology
   D policies designed to increase the attractiveness of remaining unemployed
   E more spending on transport infrastructure
2 Using an AD/AS diagram, explain why increases in business investment are encouraged by most governments.

Answers on p. 119

The economic cycle

REVISED

Although short-run growth varies across the seasons of the year, the **economic cycle** is focused on repeated patterns that occur over a number of years.

Economic cycle: the economic cycle refers to the repeated pattern of fluctuations in short-run economic growth and how it differs from the trend growth of an economy.

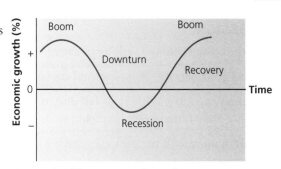

Figure 8.4 The economic cycle

The repeated phases of this cycle (also known as the business cycle or the trade cycle) can be categorised and share common characteristics in terms of macroeconomic indicators.

Boom

A boom is where short-run economic growth is above the trend growth rate (usually 3% or more).

Consumer confidence will be high with consumer spending rising quickly and consumers more willing to finance consumption through borrowed money (consumer credit).

Business confidence is high — business investment is likely to be above average.

Government finances will move either towards or further into a budget surplus.

The current account on the balance of payments will move into, or more deeply into, deficit.

Unemployment is low and falling, though firms may experience difficulties in finding skilled labour.

Inflation may be rising — often referred to as a sign of an 'overheating' economy.

Downturn

The rate of short-run growth will start to fall but may still be positive (it is likely to fall below the trend growth rate).

Business confidence will fall and investment may fall as a result.

Consumers are likely to reduce the amounts borrowed to finance consumption, and growth in consumer spending is likely to slow.

Inflation may still be above average but is likely to stop rising due to the falling demand in the economy.

Tax revenue may begin to fall due to reduced economic activity and the government's budget will move towards, or more deeply into, deficit.

Spending on imports is likely to fall and the current account balance is likely to move towards a smaller deficit or into surplus.

Unemployment will stop falling though may not rise significantly due to firms hoarding labour in case the downturn is short-lived.

Recession

Growth in the economy will be negative.

Business confidence will be low and investment will be low as a result.

Consumer spending is likely to fall due to falling incomes across the economy and rising unemployment.

Unemployment will rise and may reach high levels due to the lack of demand for output.

Inflation should fall (though it depends on the cause of inflation).

Boom: period of above average short-run economic growth.

Downturn: period where short-run economic growth falls from above average to below average.

Recession: two successive quarters of a year where short-run economic growth is negative.

Recovery: when short-run economic growth starts to increase after a recession.

The budget deficit is likely to be at its largest due to higher welfare expenditure (e.g. on unemployment benefits) and lower tax revenue being collected.

The current account balance is likely to narrow and may move into surplus due to low demand for imports.

Recovery

Short-term growth will resume and will be positive but is likely to be below the trend growth rate.

Confidence among consumers and businesses is likely to return — interest rates are likely to be low to encourage both consumption and investment.

Inflation is likely to remain low.

Unemployment is likely to remain high but will stop rising (or at least increases may slow).

The budget deficit should stop increasing (or the rate of increase will slow) as tax revenue may begin to rise.

The balance on the current account is likely to stop moving closer to a surplus.

Although these are common characteristics of each stage or phase of the economic cycle, it is worth noting that each stage is likely to be different. Unemployment in the most recent recovery period (2010 onwards) fell far earlier and to a far lower level than might have been expected.

Now test yourself

TESTED

3 State which objectives a government is likely to achieve and which it is less likely to achieve in the boom stage of the economic cycle.

Answer on p. 119

Output gaps

REVISED

Trend growth refers to the growth in the productive capacity of the economy. Short-run growth — or actual growth — will rarely be in perfect synchronisation with the trend growth rate. These differences are **output gaps**.

Output gap: the difference between actual growth and trend growth.

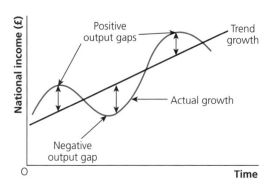

Figure 8.5 Output gaps exist when short-run growth deviates from long-run or trend growth

Output gaps can be either positive or negative:

- A positive output gap exists where actual growth is higher than trend growth.
- A negative output gap exists where actual growth is below trend growth.

Unemployment is likely to rise when the output gap is negative as the economy could produce more; therefore unemployed factors (workers and capital) will exist in the economy.

When the output gap is positive, there is greater demand for goods and services than the productive capacity of the economy allows. This is likely to lead to increases in the price level due to excess demand (i.e. inflation).

Exam tip

It is useful to note that no-one can be entirely sure what the trend growth rate is. It is based on estimates that attempt to calculate productivity improvements, increases in the labour supply and the level of productivity of new investment — none of which is easy to measure.

Revision activity

Produce a table showing how close a government is to achieving each of its objectives at each stage of the economic cycle.

Economic shocks

REVISED

Economic shocks can be favourable though most are unfavourable and are likely to have a significant impact on the ability of the government to meet its economic objectives.

There are two types of economic shocks: demand-side shocks and supply-side shocks.

Demand-side shocks

A **demand-side shock** will affect the level of national income, unemployment and inflation.

Examples of demand-side shocks include:

- the banking crisis of 2008, which affected both business and consumer confidence significantly
- an unexpectedly large change in the exchange rate or in interest rates

Supply-side shocks

A **supply-side shock** will have a knock-on effect on the willingness of firms to produce output and will lead to large changes in the level of aggregate supply.

Examples of supply-side shocks include:

- changes in commodity prices (e.g. the large oil price increases of the 1970s)
- a significant crop failure in an important product (e.g. wheat)
- a conflict in a country which produces a staple product (e.g. conflict between oil-producing countries) which limits the commodity's availability

Supply-side shocks often have more negative consequences than demand-side shocks as there is likely to be both inflation and higher unemployment if there is a sharp reduction in aggregate supply.

Economic shocks: sudden, unexpected events that will affect the macroeconomy, especially the growth rate.

Demand-side shocks: unexpected and significant changes in the level of aggregate demand.

Supply-side shocks: unexpected and significant changes in the price of factors of production or the availability of factors of production.

A demand-side shock will often only affect either unemployment or inflation but not both.

Economic shocks may have combined demand-side and supply-side effects. For example, an overseas war may have a supply-side impact on commodity prices but may also affect consumers' confidence, which has a demand-side impact.

Now test yourself

TESTED ☐

4 Using an AD/AS diagram, explain the effects of an economic shock caused by a collapse in share prices in an economy.

Answer on p. 119

Employment and unemployment

To be unemployed is to be out of work but actively seeking a job. The government's objective for unemployment is for this level (or rate) to be minimised.

Economists use the term **full employment** when describing the objective of minimising unemployment. Full employment does not mean the same as zero unemployment.

It has been estimated that even at full employment (where unemployment is said to be minimised), there may still be an unemployment rate of around 3%.

At full employment, people will still be unemployed. This occurs due to people switching jobs, businesses failing and people taking time to find vacancies that exist.

> **Full employment**: the level of employment where those who are economically active (either in work or seeking work — the same concept as the working population) can find work if they are willing to accept jobs at the going wage rate.

> **Typical mistake**
> Full employment does not mean zero unemployment.

Types of unemployment

REVISED ☐

Solving the problem of high unemployment requires appropriate economic policies.

To make the job of reducing unemployment easier, it makes sense first to classify why unemployment exists. Economists have classified unemployment into types, or causes, of unemployment.

Cyclical unemployment

Cyclical unemployment is shown on an AD/AS diagram in Figure 8.6. It occurs when AD is below the level needed to produce output at the full employment level (shown here as Y_F). It is referred to as cyclical unemployment due to the periods in the economic cycle where spending falls below the amount needed to generate full employment.

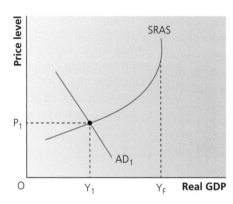

Figure 8.6 Cyclical unemployment

If spending on output is low then this means that workers who would have been producing that output will not be required and unemployment will rise. This type of unemployment is also called **demand-deficient unemployment** or **Keynesian unemployment**.

The solution to this type of unemployment will be covered later (see Chapter 9).

> **Cyclical unemployment**: unemployment caused by insufficient aggregate demand within the economy.

Frictional unemployment

Most **frictional unemployment** is short term but it can be lengthened due to lack of information, insufficient retraining opportunities or welfare benefits which are 'too generous' to provide sufficient incentive for people to take jobs sooner.

This type of unemployment can be reduced by improvements in helping people find out, on both a local and a national basis, what job vacancies exist. It is sometimes referred to as **search unemployment** due to the issue of people taking time to find the jobs that do exist.

Structural unemployment

Structural employment is due to long-term changes in the labour market which mean that certain industries are declining whilst others are growing.

Workers becoming unemployed from one industry may be unable to switch to another industry due to their not having adequate skills for the new, rising industries.

This type of unemployment is associated with occupational immobility but it is more closely connected with long-term trends in industry growth and decline.

Advances in technology may also lead to structural unemployment as workers are replaced by automated production. This type of unemployment is sometimes referred to as technological unemployment.

Structural unemployment can also result from failure to encourage people to move from one region to another, as well as the failure of regions to attract new businesses. This is also known as 'regional unemployment'.

> **Frictional unemployment**: unemployment resulting from 'friction' due to movements into and out of the job market, i.e. it occurs when people are between jobs.

> **Typical mistake**
>
> Just because there is unemployment, do not assume that there are no job vacancies. In mid-2015, there were over 700 000 vacancies for jobs.

> **Structural unemployment**: unemployment resulting from mismatches between the labour supply available and the labour demand for differently skilled labour.

> **Typical mistake**
>
> Improvements in technology cannot be blamed for rises in unemployment — they do destroy some jobs but they create more jobs than they destroy overall.

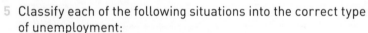

Now test yourself　　　　　　　　TESTED ☐

5　Classify each of the following situations into the correct type of unemployment:
  (a)　an unemployed steel worker who cannot find work in computer programming
  (b)　an accountant in Sheffield, unemployed due to high interest rates and government cuts
  (c)　an unemployed shop assistant unwilling to move from a rural area to a larger city
  (d)　a person leaving one job but unaware that there are plenty of similar jobs in a nearby town

Answer on p. 119

Demand-side and supply-side factors　　　REVISED ☐

The types of unemployment can also be categorised by whether they are caused by demand-side or supply-side factors.

Demand-side factors

Cyclical unemployment arises from the lack of aggregate demand, so is certainly be caused by demand-side factors.

Supply-side factors

Frictional and structural unemployment are caused by issues with the productive potential of the economy, connected with the long-term aggregate supply of an economy. They are therefore caused by supply-side factors.

In order to minimise unemployment, it is likely that governments will use a combination of policies relating to both aggregate demand and aggregate supply (see Chapter 9).

(see Chapter 9)

Now test yourself

TESTED

6 Explain why unemployment falls when the economy experiences a positive output gap.

Answer on p. 119

Answer on p. 119

Global factors

REVISED

Structural unemployment can also be increased by global factors. Many emerging industrial nations are able to produce goods at a much lower cost than they can be produced in the UK. This makes the foreign goods much more price competitive, which is likely to lead to a decline in these manufacturing industries in the UK. As a result, unemployment in these industries is likely to rise in the UK and the workers will remain unemployed unless they are able fill vacancies in other industries in which the UK has an advantage.

Inflation and deflation

Inflation was a very common problem in the UK during the twentieth century. However, since the recession of the early 1990s, it has been less so. In recent years, in both the UK and the rest of Europe, governments have increasingly begun to worry about deflation. Both inflation and **deflation** are problematic but for different reasons.

- **Inflation** refers to the annual increase in the general level of prices. The price level in the UK is measured by the consumer price index (CPI).
- **Deflation** refers to the situation where the general level of prices is falling over time. The UK briefly experienced deflation (as measured by the CPI) in 2015. This means that the 'inflation basket' of goods and services was actually cheaper to buy for a period in 2015 than it would have been one year earlier in 2014.
- **Disinflation** refers to the concept of a falling rate of inflation (e.g. where inflation falls from 5% to 2%).

> **Deflation**: a fall in the average level of prices over time.
>
> **Disinflation**: where the rate of inflation is falling but is still positive.

> **Typical mistake**
>
> Falling inflation does not mean that goods and services are getting cheaper — there is still inflation. What it means is that the rate at which prices are increasing is slowing down — a situation known as disinflation.

Now test yourself

TESTED

7 Explain the difference between deflation and low inflation.

Answer on p. 120

Answer on p. 120

Causes of inflation

In economic theory, there are two main causes of inflation:
● **demand-pull inflation**
● **cost-push inflation**

Demand-pull inflation

High levels of spending give signals to firms to increase output, but as we get closer to the capacity level of the economy (as dictated by the vertical LRAS curve), the higher spending will lead to firms increasing their prices as they incur higher costs in producing more output. Eventually, in the long run, when the economy is operating on the LRAS, any increase in AD will lead only to inflation, rather than to increases in output.

In Figure 8.7, growth in AD from AD_1 to AD_4 increases output but eventually leads to demand-pull inflation, shown here by increasingly large rises in the price level from P_1 to P_4.

The solution to reducing demand-pull inflation is to reduce the level of aggregate demand by reducing any of the components that the government can influence, as this would ease upward pressure on prices.

Cost-push inflation

If any of the costs of production increase, then the rise in costs will reduce a firm's profit margin unless it increases the selling price, thus leading to higher prices. (If firms accepted a lower profit margin when faced with rising costs, cost-push inflation might not occur.)

A fall in the exchange rate will lead to higher costs for imported materials and therefore this can lead to cost-push inflation. (Inflation caused by a falling exchange rate is sometimes referred to as 'imported inflation'.)

As Figure 8.8 shows, a leftward shift in the SRAS curve from $SRAS_1$ to $SRAS_2$ will lead to higher prices caused by cost-push factors. It will also lead to a lower equilibrium output level.

In this way, cost-push inflation leads not only to higher prices but also to falling output (and likely rises in unemployment at the same time). This combination of problems is referred to as 'stagflation' – stagnant growth in national output and inflation occurring together.

> **Demand-pull inflation**: inflation caused by excessively high levels of aggregate demand beyond that needed to generate full employment.
>
> **Cost-push inflation**: inflation that occurs due to rises in the costs of production incurred by firms.

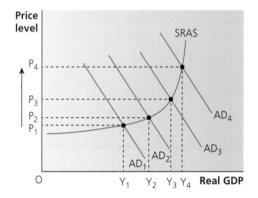

Figure 8.7 Growth in AD and its impact on demand-pull inflation

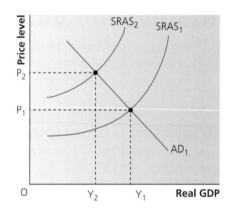

Figure 8.8 The impact of a leftward shift in SRAS

8 Using AS/AD diagrams, explain how deflation can be caused by changes in both aggregate demand and aggregate supply.

Answer on p. 120

Commodity prices and inflation

Commodity prices are volatile and as a result **commodities** are often traded for the purposes of making profits through speculation on future price changes.

Oil prices have a significant effect on the inflation rate due to oil's importance as an input to industrial production (it is used not only to transport goods and workers, but also to make goods such as plastics).

Oil-producing nations often coordinate production decisions so as to restrict the quantity of oil being produced and this reduction in supply leads to large increases in oil prices (due to demand being very price inelastic). This can result in sharp rises in inflation, as happened in the UK on more than one occasion in the 1970s (peaking at around 25% inflation in 1975).

> **Commodity**: a homogeneous product (all output of the product is identical) that is often used as a basic input into production. Common examples are oil, copper, minerals, cotton and basic foodstuffs (e.g. wheat and cocoa).

Impact of other economies on UK inflation

The UK is a fairly **open economy**. This means that changes in other economies can affect inflation in the UK in a number of ways:

- Growth in foreign economies will increase the demand for UK exports. This in theory could lead to demand-pull inflation (though most demand-pull inflation is caused by excessive growth in consumption rather than exports).
- Similarly, recessions in our major trading partners will ease demand-pull pressure due to reduced spending on UK exports.
- Increased growth in overseas economies will lead to more demand for commodities and other basic production materials. This increased demand will push up prices of these goods and the UK may experience cost-push inflation as a result.
- Changes in the exchange rate between different currencies will also affect inflation. Falls in the exchange rate will lead to cost-push pressure as import prices rise.

> **Open economy**: an economy in which foreign trade accounts for a significant proportion of GDP.

The balance of payments on current account

Foreign trade is important for the UK. Jobs and income are derived from our ability to export goods and services to other countries, with additional multiplier effects. Imports are also important, as they allow consumers access to products they could not otherwise obtain, or could not obtain at a reasonable price. Although imported goods and services do not contribute directly to our national income, they supply our firms with vital inputs into the production process. All these transactions are recorded in the balance of payments.

The balance of payments is divided into three sections:
- current account
- capital account
- financial account

> **Exam tip**
> It is only the current account of the balance of payments that we are concerned with at AS.

The current account is concerned with the flows of income from trade, the use of factors of production and other transfers between countries. It looks at earnings made by the use of assets rather than the assets themselves.

The current account consists of these sections:
- **trade in goods** — exports and imports of goods
- **trade in services** — exports and imports of services
- **primary income** — net investment incomes
- **secondary income** — transfers of money between countries

Trade in goods

The balance of trade in goods calculates the value of goods exported by the UK less the value of goods imported by the UK.

The UK typically runs a fairly large deficit on the trade in goods balance.

The balance on the trade in goods is sometimes known as the 'visible' balance.

Trade in services

The balance of trade in services calculates the value of services exported by the UK less the value of services imported by the UK.

The UK typically runs a surplus on trade in services, though this is not as large as the deficit on the trade in goods balance.

Major services exported by the UK relate to the UK's financial services industry (e.g. banking and insurance).

This balance is refered to as the 'invisible' balance.

Primary income

Primary income refers to the net investment income flows earned by the UK.

This is calculated as investment income received from abroad less any investment income paid abroad.

Investment income relates to the earnings from assets located outside the UK. This includes earnings on financial assets, such as dividends and interest earned from overseas, as well as the profits and wages paid by UK-owned direct investments in businesses located overseas.

The inward flow of investment income will be accompanied by an outward flow of investment income, which relates to foreigners who own assets located in the UK. The inward flow of income less the outward flow of income gives the net investment income position.

The balance on net investment income in the UK used to be a large surplus but this has moved into deficit recently.

The deficit on net investment income is explained by rapid growth in investment in the UK by investors in countries like China and India (thus creating flows of investment income back to those countries).

> **Primary income**: flows of income from investments abroad less flows of income from foreign investments located in the UK.

Secondary income

Secondary income refers to the transfers of money between countries. This usually arises from:

- private transfers, e.g. wages of overseas workers sent back to their family at home
- foreign aid
- grants
- gifts

The biggest two components of the current account are the trade in goods and the trade in services. The deficit on goods outweighs the surplus on services, which means that overall the current account balance is normally in deficit.

Now test yourself

TESTED

9 Decide whether each of the following transactions would improve or worsen a current account deficit:
   (a) sale of goods abroad
   (b) wages paid by workers overseas sent back to families in the UK
   (c) purchase of services provided by a French investment bank
   (d) UK tourists on holiday in Greece
   (e) aid given to developing countries
   (f) dividends received by UK residents on shares held in a German company

Answer on p. 120

Balance on the current account

REVISED

Factors determining exports

Foreign GDP

As foreign GDP rises, spending in those countries will also rise and this will lead to a greater demand for UK goods and services (i.e. they will import more as their spending increases).

Productivity

If UK productivity rises relative to foreign productivity, this means UK firms can produce more output for a proportionately smaller amount of inputs. This increased efficiency will mean that costs per unit of output fall, which allows firms to price their goods more competitively compared with foreign substitutes. This should boost the demand for UK goods — thus leading to increases in exports.

Inflation

If UK inflation is higher than foreign inflation, it means that the prices of UK goods are rising faster than those of goods produced overseas. This means UK goods will become less price competitive and foreign buyers will switch away from buying UK goods — thus leading to lower exports.

The main issue here is not the rate of inflation, but the level of relative inflation (i.e. UK inflation compared with foreign inflation).

Exchange rates

A stronger pound will buy more foreign currency. However, this also means that foreigners will need more of their own currency to buy the same amount of sterling. This means a stronger (or higher) exchange rate will lead to lower demand for UK exports due to them appearing more expensive in foreign currency terms. Similarly, a weaker pound should lead to a higher volume of exports as these goods will now appear cheaper in foreign currency terms.

Factors determining imports

UK GDP

As UK GDP rises, spending in the UK rises — especially on consumption. The amount of goods and services imported will rise along with consumption as households spend their higher incomes. Thus, although a high growth rate of GDP may be good for the economy in a number of ways, it will lead to a higher volume of imports and a deteriorating trade balance on the current account.

Exchange rate

A strong pound buys more foreign currency, which means foreign goods can be bought for a smaller amount of sterling. This means that imports are cheaper and as a consequence their volume will rise.

Many of the factors mentioned earlier which affect the demand for exports will also affect the demand for UK imports. For example, relatively higher UK inflation will lead to lower demand for UK exports but will also increase the demand for imports in the UK as foreign goods will appear relatively cheap to buy.

Similarly, if UK productivity is low compared with foreign productivity then, by the same reasoning, demand for imports in the UK may rise due to those goods becoming relatively cheaper (due to foreign firms being more cost efficient).

> **Typical mistake**
>
> Do not assume that UK economic growth will generate more exports. Exports are purchased by those overseas so it is growth in these countries that will boost exports.

> **Exam tip**
>
> Remember that even if exports appear more or less competitive in terms of price, there are other, non-price, factors which will determine the level of demand for them. Consider the price elasticity of demand for the type of good.

Possible conflicts between macroeconomic policy objectives

As stated in Chapter 6, the UK government has a number of macroeconomic policy objectives. The key objectives are:
- economic growth (positive but stable growth in GDP)
- price stability (an inflation target of 2%)
- minimising unemployment
- stable balance of payments on current account (mainly between exports and imports)
- balancing the budget (between government spending and taxation)

Output gaps

REVISED

An output gap occurs when the actual (short-run) growth rate differs from the trend (long-run) growth rate. These can be negative output gaps or positive output gaps (see Figure 8.5 on p. 89).

Negative output gaps

These occur when actual growth is below trend growth.

If there is a negative output gap then cyclical unemployment is likely to increase.

As growth is below the productive capacity of the economy, there will be resources (workers and capital) which are not required for production. This means that workers will become unemployed.

Unemployment can rise in this way even if actual growth is positive; if the trend growth for the economy is 2% and actual growth is only 1% then this means that fewer workers are needed given that each worker, on average, can produce 2% more each year — and only a 1% increase in output is needed.

The negative output gap can also be shown on an AD/AS diagram (see Figure 8.9). This type of unemployment can best be solved by increasing the level of aggregate demand.

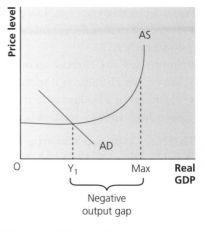

Figure 8.9 A negative output gap is caused here by insufficient AD

Positive output gaps

These occur when actual growth is above trend growth.

A positive output gap will eventually lead to rising prices, i.e. higher inflation.

With a positive output gap, although output is temporarily higher than its trend rate, this cannot be maintained in the long run. In order to keep output at this higher level, firms will find costs increasing (such as paying higher wages to attract workers) and this will lead to inflationary pressures.

The positive output gap can be shown on an AD/AS diagram (see Figure 8.10). This type of inflation can best be solved by decreasing the level of aggregate demand.

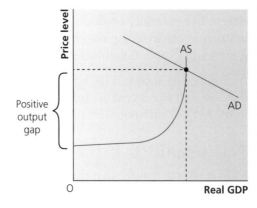

Figure 8.10 A positive output gap here generates inflationary pressure in the economy

Now test yourself

TESTED

10 What are the characteristics of a negative output gap and a positive output gap?

Answer on p. 119

Policy conflicts

REVISED

As we can see, two of the main macroeconomic objectives (inflation and unemployment) require different solutions — one requires more and one requires less aggregate demand. This is described as a policy conflict.

A policy conflict exists when attempts to solve one economic problem lead away from solving another problem. We can examine potential conflicts by looking at how certain objectives might be achieved.

Policy objectives needing increased aggregate demand:
● short-run economic growth (spending and income are closely connected)
● reducing cyclical unemployment (jobs depend on the level of spending)
● eliminating a budget deficit (this is easier with higher spending, which means more taxes are collected)

Policy objectives needing lower aggregate demand:
- reducing demand-pull inflation (this inflation is caused by there being too much AD)
- improving the current account balance (this will occur if imports are lower, which follows if spending falls)
- eliminating a budget deficit (this may require lower government spending, though some would dispute this)

Therefore, conflicts will arise between objectives that need higher AD and those that need lower AD. Common conflicts arise between:
- minimising unemployment and keeping inflation low and stable
- increasing economic growth and achieving balance on the current account
- reducing the budget deficit through cuts in government spending, and achieving economic growth and minimising unemployment

Remember, these conflicts can be made worse by multiplier effects. For example, a reduction in government spending in order to close the gap on a budget deficit may lead to a significantly larger fall in national income as a result.

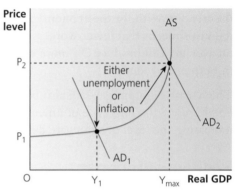

Figure 8.11 The conflict resulting from relying on policies that affect AD only

As Figure 8.11 shows, if we rely only on policies that affect AD, then we will face a conflict between experiencing unemployment (with AD_1) or inflation (with AD_2).

Policy conflicts in the long run

Most economists agree that there are policy conflicts in the short run at least. However, some would argue that these conflicts do not have to occur in the long run.

Different policies can be used to address different problems, which may minimise the conflict that exists. In the long run, the economy should be operating on the LRAS, meaning that there is no cyclical unemployment in the long run. If there is no cyclical unemployment, then there is no need for higher AD.

Supply-side policies may be the solution to the trade-off that exists between inflation and unemployment in the short run — these are explored in the next chapter.

There are other conflicts that exist in trying to ensure an equitable distribution of income. Some economists argue that higher growth can be achieved if governments do not worry about unequal distribution of income, and that by cutting taxes for high earners, higher growth can be achieved. This point is open to debate, though.

Another argument is that cutting welfare benefits will reduce unemployment and will improve long-run growth. Again, this would conflict with the objective of an equitable distribution of income.

Revision activity

Draw AD/AS diagrams to illustrate the issues of cyclical unemployment and both types of inflation, and add notes on the effect of these on the achievement of other government objectives.

Now test yourself

TESTED

11 Explain why there may be a conflict between inflation and unemployment.

Answer on p. 119

Exam practice

In 2011, UK inflation was close to 5%. This is significantly above its target level. However, despite this, the Bank of England chose not to raise interest rates. The reason given for not raising rates was that the high inflation was caused by the fall in the pound's value, a recent rise in commodity prices and a recent rise in VAT. The governor of the Bank of England believed that without these factors, inflation would have been below its target level of 2%.

1 Define the term 'disinflation'. [3]
2 Briefly explain how inflation is calculated in the UK. [6]
3 Explain how two factors mentioned in the extract are leading to higher inflation. [6]
4 Using an AD/AS diagram, analyse the effects on economic performance of the factors mentioned in the extract. [10]   ONLINE ☐

Summary

You should have an understanding of:
- The distinction between short-run and long-run growth as well as the factors contributing to each type of growth.
- The features of each stage of the economic cycle and how to describe them.
- How differences in short-run and long-run growth lead to output gaps.

- The methods of measurement and the factors that determine each of the following macroeconomic indicators:
  – unemployment
  – inflation
  – current account on the balance of payments
- The policy conflicts that arise in attempting to achieve multiple objectives, both in the short run and in the long run.

Answers and quick quizzes online

Monetary policy

The main focus of **monetary policy** is on the level of interest rates set in the economy. Other aspects of monetary policy include the size of the money supply, the availability of credit (i.e. money that can be borrowed by consumers and businesses) and the exchange rate of the currency.

Monetary policy is the job of the central bank of the economy, which in the UK is the Bank of England. Since 1997, the Bank of England has been largely free of government control in setting monetary policy.

This does not mean that the government has no influence: it still sets the targets for the Bank of England to achieve, and it still reserves the right to intervene in the management of monetary policy in special circumstances, such as in the financial crisis of 2008.

> **Monetary policy**: the manipulation of the price and availability of money within an economy to achieve economic policy objectives.

Objectives of monetary policy

REVISED

The key aim of UK monetary policy is to achieve the government's inflation target — using the CPI measurement of inflation — at a rate of 2% (plus or minus 1%) per year. Other objectives of government policy, such as full employment and steady economic growth, are important but should be pursued using monetary policy only if they do not conflict with the inflation target.

The inflation target of 2% is achieved through changes to the **Bank rate**. Decisions over the level at which to set bank rate are made monthly by the Bank of England's Monetary Policy Committee.

> **Bank rate**: the interest rate set by the Bank of England that affects interest rates set by banks and other financial institutions such as building societies across the economy.

> **Exam tip**
>
> Although interest rates affect the reward for savings, the main effect of interest rate changes considered in economics is the change in the cost of borrowing.

Now test yourself

TESTED

1 Explain three ways in which aggregate demand would be affected by a cut in interest rates.

Answer on p. 120

The Monetary Policy Committee

Monetary policy is mainly effected by changes in the level of interest rates. The level of interest rates is set by the **Monetary Policy Committee** of the Bank of England.

The MPC will consider how a range of economic factors will impact on the UK inflation rate. Areas of economic performance that will be considered include:
- consumer spending and consumer confidence
- business investment and business confidence
- fiscal policy — government expenditure and taxation
- the exchange rate
- commodity prices
- unemployment and labour market conditions

> **Monetary Policy Committee**: this currently consists of nine members and meets monthly to consider recent developments and likely future developments of aspects of UK economic performance.

The MPC will consider whether the economic conditions currently facing the UK, and those that are likely to face the UK in the short and medium term, are likely to either increase or decrease the inflation rate over the next 2 years. This will be achieved by assessing how changes in the economic environment will affect both aggregate demand and aggregate supply.

If there are increased chances of inflation rising in the near future, then it is likely that members of the MPC will vote to raise interest rates. This is because a higher level of interest rates is likely to lead to lower aggregate demand which will, in turn, lead to lower pressure on demand-pull inflation.

The opposite would also be true; and if there is likely to be downward pressure on prices, then members of the MPC are more likely to lower interest rates to stimulate the level of aggregate demand.

For example, a rise in the Bank rate is likely to have the following effects on the UK economy:
- lower levels of borrowing by consumers
- higher monthly repayments for those with variable rate mortgages
- increased incentives for households to save
- lower investment by businesses as the profitability of investment projects is reduced
- a rise in the exchange rate, causing UK exports to be less competitive, but imports to be cheaper, thus potentially reducing cost-push inflation as well.

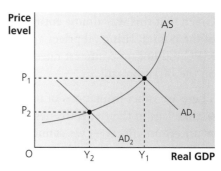

Figure 9.1 The effects of raising interest rates

All these effects will reduce the level of aggregate demand and should lead to a reduction in demand-pull inflation. In Figure 9.1, increases in interest rates will lead to a shift from AD_1 to AD_2, which is likely to bring down inflation but lower economic growth and increase unemployment.

It is worth bearing in mind that changes in interest rates usually take over a year (and perhaps up to 2 years) to work through the economy fully. This means the changes should be forward looking and the MPC should consider where inflation will be in 1–2 years' time.

Changing interest rates in response to rises in the rate of inflation is probably too late — the changes should happen well in advance. This gap in time is referred to as a **time lag**.

> **Exam tip**
>
> Changes in interest rates are not guaranteed to work immediately or exactly as planned. Remember that the predicted effects are based on consumer behaviour, which is not always predictable.

This is made harder because the data on which interest rate changes are based may take some months to become available: at any time, we may be looking at data which are at least 1 month old, if not older.

The effect of interest rates on other objectives

REVISED

There will be a policy conflict when using interest rates to reduce the rate of inflation. Higher interest rates should lead to lower inflation through the transmission mechanism of lower aggregate demand. However, the lower level of aggregate demand will have the following effects:

- higher unemployment caused by lack of spending
- lower short-term economic growth due to reduced demand
- growth of the supply side of the economy is limited due to lack of investment in productive capacity
- lower tax revenue collected due to lower economic activity
- reduced levels of exports due to a likely rise in the exchange rate, which has effects on economic growth and unemployment

Limitations of interest rates in controlling the economy

REVISED

Though the main impact of higher interest rates is on aggregate demand, there is some effect on aggregate supply, but this is less significant and less certain in terms of the size of its impact. This means that interest rates are less useful as a means of controlling rises in cost-push inflation.

In 2012, UK inflation rose well above its target level, reaching over 5%. Given that this was almost entirely due to cost-push factors (falling value of the pound, rising oil prices and rises in indirect taxes), however, the MPC did not raise interest rates as it was felt it would have little impact on the inflation rate.

There are other limitations of using interest rates to control the economy:

- time lags in their effectiveness
- uncertain effects — we cannot be sure of their impact
- when interest rates are low, further cuts may not be possible
- changes may have to be large to have any significant effect (most changes in interest rate are in steps of +/− 0.25%)

Now test yourself

TESTED

2 Explain why the MPC might decrease interest rates even if the latest month's inflation rate has increased.

Answer on p. 120

Interest rates and the exchange rate

REVISED

A change in interest rates is likely to affect the exchange rate.

A rise in interest rate is likely to lead to a rise in the value of the pound on the foreign exchange markets. This occurs because a higher interest rate will attract flows of speculative short-term money (often known as 'hot money') into that currency due to the higher returns that can now be obtained. The higher demand for the currency leads to an increase in its value.

The currency's higher value will lead to downward pressure on cost-push inflation, as a higher exchange rate will lead to lower prices for imported goods and lower costs for those businesses that import materials for use in production.

The link between interest rates and the exchange rate is not as clear as the link between interest rates and aggregate demand. It will depend on what is happening to interest rates in other economies at the same time and how expected the change in interest rates was.

> **Typical mistake**
>
> The link between interest rates and exchange rates is often unclear. If an increase in interest rates is widely expected, the rise in the exchange rate may occur earlier, anticipating rather than following the change.

The effects of exchange rate changes on other macroeconomic policy objectives

REVISED

Changes in the exchange rate, whether caused by changes in interest rates or not, will affect other objectives in a number of ways:
- A rise in the exchange rate will lead to exports becoming less price competitive in foreign markets.
- A fall in the exchange rate will boost exports, leading to more jobs in the export sector.
- A fall in the exchange rate will lead to higher inflation as imported goods and services will become more expensive.
- An unstable exchange rate will make it hard for UK exporters to plan levels of production. It will also make foreign consumers less willing to buy UK goods due to uncertainty over prices, unless UK producers are willing to absorb the changes in their profit margins by accepting a fixed price, measured in foreign currency terms.

> **Typical mistake**
>
> A fall in the exchange rate will make imports more expensive but this doesn't mean UK consumers will switch away from buying imports — at least not in the short run.

Fiscal policy

Fiscal policy involves making deliberate changes in either government spending or taxation. Government spending is generally financed by the collection of taxation revenue. The difference between the level of government spending and the tax collected is referred to as the budget balance.

Given that the government spends huge sums of money (over £750 billion in 2015–16), it would be highly unusual if it managed to spend the exact amount collected in tax revenue. Each year there will be either a deficit or a surplus. In the last 40 years, there has been a surplus in around 5 years only, with the deficit becoming increasingly large in the last 10 years.

Budget deficits are financed by borrowing. The government issues **bonds** (a form of IOU) that people purchase from the government, which enable the excess spending to be financed. The bond will pay the holder a fixed rate of interest until it has to be repaid. Typically bonds have a 10-year life before they are repaid.

> **Exam tip**
>
> The term 'stance' is often used to describe the general effect of a policy on activity. For example, an expansionary monetary stance would be used to describe monetary policy that is promoting faster growth.

> **Fiscal policy**: fiscal policy involves deliberate changes in either government spending or taxation.
>
> **Bonds**: a method of financing a budget deficit, bonds are issued by the government to people who lend the government money and receive interest payments in return, plus the eventual repayment of the bond.

> **Typical mistake**
>
> Cutting taxes should boost economic activity, but do not assume the tax cut to be self-financing; the boost in economic activity will not lead to tax revenues rising *in excess* of the tax cut.

Fiscal policy and the national debt

REVISED

Any time the government runs a budget deficit as part of its fiscal policy, it will have to borrow the shortfall. As stated earlier, this is done through the issue of debt in the form of interest-bearing government bonds. These bonds will eventually be repaid, but until that date, they form part of the **national debt**.

> **National debt**: the stock of all outstanding government debt that has yet to be repaid.

At any one time, the government is likely to be paying back past debt as bonds reach their maturity date (repayment date), but as stated earlier, budget deficits occur much more frequently than budget surpluses. As a result, even as debt is repaid, more debt is taken on, meaning that the national debt does not necessarily shrink.

It is this outstanding debt on which interest has to be paid each year. In 2015–16, around £50 billion will be spent by the government on these interest payments.

The size of the national debt is high when compared with the national income (it is normal to express national debt as a percentage of national income), but this is not necessarily worrying: most households, for example, regularly fund house purchases with mortgages that are in excess of the households' annual income. The UK national debt is currently around £1.6 trillion (or £1600 billion). This is equivalent to almost 90% of the UK's GDP.

> **Typical mistake**
>
> Do not confuse the national debt with the budget deficit; the budget deficit adds to the national debt, but the debt will still be there even if there is a budget surplus.

Any budget deficit will add to this debt. At the same time, any budget surpluses will allow the government to pay off existing debts and therefore the national debt will fall.

Why do we appear always to run deficits? This is largely due to the popularity of government spending among voters. People like well-funded schools and hospitals, and good roads. Few politicians would get elected if they promised tax rises. If the debt is to be paid off some years in the future, politicians seeking election today are unlikely to worry.

> **Exam tip**
>
> Think about why budget deficits are so commonplace.

Now test yourself

TESTED

3 Why will national debt as a percentage of national income fall even if the government runs continual budget deficits?

Answer on p. 120

Taxation

REVISED

Taxation revenue collected by the government finances government expenditure. In general, the following types of tax exist.

Direct taxation

Direct taxes are normally placed on incomes and are often taken away by the employer before the employee ever receives them; self-employed workers pay tax themselves.

> **Direct tax**: a direct tax is one that cannot be passed on to another person and is usually levied on incomes.

Common examples of direct taxes in the UK are as follows:
- **income tax** — based on a percentage of earnings above a set tax-free threshold

- **national insurance contributions (NICs)** — paid by workers to cover state benefit entitlements
- **corporation tax** — paid by companies based on their reported profits

Indirect taxation

Common examples of **indirect taxes** in the UK are:
- **value added tax (VAT)** — currently 20% on most items (though some goods are 'zero rated')
- **excise duties** — taxes on particular items, such as petrol, alcohol and tobacco

In the UK, the three main taxes used are income tax (around 25% of tax receipts), VAT (around 20% of tax receipts) and NICs (also around 20% of tax receipts).

> **Indirect tax**: a tax on spending. It is termed indirect because the seller can pass on the tax to the buyer, i.e. the seller can avoid the tax by increasing the selling price, though it cannot always be passed on in full.

> **Exam tip**
>
> When writing about taxes, be clear to distinguish between the rate of tax and the revenue raised by a tax — they are connected but different.

Progressive, regressive and proportional taxation

REVISED

One objective of the government is to create a favourable distribution of income. This involves ensuring that the gap between the richest and the poorest households is less than it might be if left to the market. Inequality may be seen as undesirable if it becomes too great. As a result, governments regularly use the taxation system to create a more equitable distribution of income.

Progressive taxes

Progressive taxation is achieved by having different tax bands. In the UK, the current tax bands are as follows:

Tax rates for 2015/16	Income range (£)
Tax-free allowance	0–10600
Basic rate of 20%	10600–42385
Higher rate of 40%	42385+
Additional rate of 45%	150000+

> **Progressive taxes**: where those on higher incomes pay a higher proportion of their income in tax compared with those on lower incomes.

Those earning above £100000 would see their personal allowance gradually reduced until it is withdrawn fully, depending on their earnings.

What makes this system of tax progressive is that it is paid only on any additional income earned. For example, a person earning over £42385 would pay 40% only on their earnings above that level. On the income earned below that, they would pay 20%, apart from £10600 on which they would pay no tax at all.

This means that low earners pay a relatively low rate of tax: someone earning around £15000 would pay only £880 in income tax, a rate of less than 6%.

At the other end, the rates paid by above-average earners rise from 20% to 40% and higher if they earn very large amounts. Hence, the income of above-average earners reduces more quickly than that of below-average earners.

Now test yourself

TESTED

4 (a) Based on the table of different tax bands for the UK shown on page 107, calculate how much income tax someone would pay if they earned:
  (i) £15 000
  (ii) £30 000
  (iii) £45 000
  (b) Express the amounts paid in tax by each of the people described in question 4(a) above as a percentage of their income — this gives you the average rate of tax paid by that person.
  (c) What do the answers in (b) tell you about the UK system of income tax?

Answer on p. 120

Regressive taxes

An example of a **regressive tax** in the UK was the 'community charge', which existed before the council tax was introduced. Every person had to pay the same amount, regardless of income. The tax was seen as very controversial as it hit the poorest earners harder.

> **Regressive taxes**: taxes that increase in relative size on lower income earners.

Some think VAT is also a regressive tax but this would be true only if it were charged on items that poorer earners have to buy in the same quantities as others in the population. This is one reason why food is exempt from VAT: if food were subject to VAT, it would account for a higher proportion of a poorer earner's income.

Proportional taxes

Economists sometimes refer to **proportional taxes** as 'flat taxes'. A tax with one uniform percentage rate and no tax-free thresholds would fall into this category. VAT can be seen as proportional if it is on non-essential items (items that poorer households do not have to buy in the same quantities as others).

> **Proportional taxes**: taxes that are paid in equal proportions by everyone.

> **Typical mistake**
>
> A progressive tax doesn't just mean that rich people pay more tax — they would pay more even if the tax were proportional. What it means is that they pay *proportionately* more.

Now test yourself

TESTED

5 Why do some people think VAT is a regressive tax?

Answer on p. 120

Fiscal policy and aggregate demand

Changes in the government's fiscal stance, i.e. changes in either tax or government spending, will affect aggregate demand. Changes to AD resulting from fiscal policy are sometimes referred to as 'demand management'.

Expansionary fiscal policy would refer to either increases in government spending or reductions in taxation, or to both. This will shift the AD curve to the right.

Contractionary fiscal policy will shift the AD curve to the left.

As a component of AD, changes in government spending will directly affect the overall total of AD.

As we know, changes in AD, whether caused by changes in government spending or not, will change the following macroeconomic indicators:
- the level of real GDP
- the level of unemployment
- the price level

There will be multiplier effects caused by the change in government spending, which are also likely to affect the macroeconomic indicators mentioned above.

> **Exam tip**
>
> The terms 'tight' or 'loose' are sometimes used to describe 'contractionary' and 'expansionary' policies, both monetary and fiscal.

> **Revision activity**
>
> Produce AD/AS diagrams for both contractionary and expansionary fiscal and monetary policy.

Effects of changes in tax

Changes in taxes on incomes will affect the disposable income of households (income after tax deductions), which will affect the level of consumption — higher taxes act to reduce consumption.

Changes in taxes on business profits will affect the level of investment as they reduce the funds available for investment in the business.

Again, there will be multiplier effects. These will be less certain. For example, a tax cut which increases disposable incomes may not always lead to higher consumption; households may decide to save some of this extra income, or spend it on imports.

As with government spending, whether or not the fiscal policy is designed to increase AD (through lower taxes) or reduce AD (through higher taxes), there will be potential effects on real GDP, unemployment and the price level.

> **Exam tip**
>
> Changes in tax can influence behaviour but will not always have a precisely predictable effect — a cut in income tax may simply encourage households to save more. Be careful of making snap judgements.

Fiscal policy and aggregate supply

Change in fiscal policy can also have effects on the aggregate supply curve (both the SRAS and the LRAS curves).

Effects of changes in indirect taxes

Increases in any indirect tax, such as VAT or excise duties, which affect businesses will shift the SRAS curve to the left, and reductions will shift it to the right.

This is because higher indirect taxes cannot always be fully passed on to the consumer in the form of higher prices. Thus, the firm's profit margins drop per unit sold.

This reduces the incentive for firms to supply output at any given price level.

Supply-side fiscal policies

Fiscal policy deliberately designed to affect aggregate supply is often referred to as **supply-side fiscal policy**. Common examples of supply-side fiscal policies include:

- Targeted government spending on improvements to the economy's production capacity, shifting the LRAS curve to the right. This would involve spending on infrastructure, such as transport networks, or subsidising investment in new technology.
- Tax incentives can be given to firms to encourage them either to take on more workers, or to spend more on investment. For example, corporation tax in the UK has been steadily reduced by the government to attract more firms to set up in the UK.
- Reducing direct taxation (especially income tax) to make work more attractive.

> **Supply-side fiscal policies:** policies that involve changes in fiscal policy that are designed to improve the LRAS of the economy.

Now test yourself

TESTED

6 Show on an AD/AS diagram how a cut in income tax can have two effects on the economy.

Answer on p. 120

Fiscal policy and microeconomics

REVISED

Fiscal policy can also be seen as having microeconomic effects where it involves intervention in individual markets.

Government spending on subsidies can encourage consumption or production of certain desirable products (e.g. merit goods like education and health).

Indirect taxes can be used to discourage consumption and production of certain products (e.g. demerit goods like cigarettes).

Often these microeconomic interventions are intended to change the pattern of economic activity. For example, if an industry is in decline and a new one is set to replace it, the government may speed up the growth of the new industry through subsidies, such as the UK government subsidising solar panels to encourage households to install them.

High indirect taxes on an industry will also affect the success of those businesses. For example, some blame the high excise duty on beer for the closure of many pubs (whereas others blame this on the smoking ban introduced in pubs and other venues in 2007).

Supply-side policies

The supply side of the economy refers to the level of aggregate supply, both short term and long term. This is connected with the productive capacity of the economy (i.e. how much can be produced over time). Factors of production, such as labour, as well as the quantity of capital stock (buildings, machinery, infrastructure) will determine how much can be produced.

Successful **supply-side policies** will shift the LRAS to the right, allowing for expansion of AD without upward pressure on prices emerging. In Figure 9.2, we can see output increase from Y_1 to Y_2 but there is no change in the price level.

> **Supply-side policies:** deliberate actions taken by the government designed to increase the LRAS of the economy (i.e. shift the LRAS curve to the right).

Exam practice answers and quick quizzes at **www.hoddereducation.co.uk/myrevisionnotes**

If successful, supply-side policies increase the amount that an economy can produce without inflationary pressures emerging. By increasing the potential output level, more can be produced before there is upward pressure on prices.

Many (but not all) supply-side policies are microeconomic in origin. This means the policy may concentrate on one particular market or one particular industry, rather than the economy as a whole.

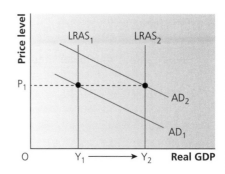

Figure 9.2 Impact of successful supply-side policies

Supply-side improvements

REVISED

We should distinguish between supply-side policies and **supply-side improvements**. Whereas supply-side policies are direct action taken by the government to improve the productive capacity of the economy, supply-side improvements are slightly different.

Firms themselves have a desire to increase output (if possible) and this can be seen as a natural consequence of allowing markets to work reasonably freely.

Having said that, direct supply-side policies adopted by the government will also lead to supply-side improvements in the economy.

> **Supply-side improvements:** these arise out of general increases in the productive capacity resulting from businesses acting out of their own interest in improving efficiency and the quantity of their output.

> **Typical mistake**
> Improvements in the supply-side of the economy can occur without action being taken by the government.

Taxation and supply-side policy

REVISED

One major area of supply-side policy relates to the government's policy on taxation.

Direct taxes on incomes can be seen as acting as a disincentive for people to work. The higher that income is taxed, the less attractive work becomes as it will mean more income is taken by the government.

Supply-side economists believe that reducing taxes on incomes will encourage employed people to work longer hours, as they keep more of their income and encourage unemployed people to take jobs, given that lower taxes on incomes will make jobs seem more worthwhile. We know that income tax cuts, as part of fiscal policy, will boost output through higher AD, but they may also lead to higher output through higher AS if more people want to work.

In the UK and other economies there has been a deliberate move away from taxing incomes towards indirect taxes. The standard rate of income tax in the UK has fallen from 33% in the late 1970s to 20% today.

In addition, the amount of income one can earn before paying any tax has also risen significantly in recent years. This should make people more willing to take jobs and less willing to remain unemployed. In short, it makes work financially more attractive.

Furthermore, cuts in corporation tax should also act as a supply-side policy. This occurs by encouraging businesses to spend more on investment, thus expanding the UK's economic capacity. Lower corporation taxes have also attracted foreign firms to locate in the UK.

7 Give reasons why lower income tax might not lead to more people working longer hours.

Answer on p. 120

Labour market supply-side policies

REVISED

Many supply-side policies are put into action in reforms to the labour market. The labour market deals with the interaction between labour supply (workers) and labour demand (firms looking to produce output).

The purpose of labour market supply-side policies is to create a more **flexible labour market**. This means reducing the barriers to entry into different labour markets — making it easier for people to enter the labour market as a whole and to swap between different labour markets in different industries. Labour market supply-side policies include those listed below.

> **Flexible labour market**: where there are few barriers to firms hiring and firing workers as required.

Reductions in income tax

See the section 'Taxation and supply-side policy' on p. 111.

Reductions in welfare benefits

Making work financially more attractive will encourage people away from unemployment and into job vacancies. Coupled with this is the policy to make it less financially attractive to be unemployed. This involves making it harder to qualify for welfare benefits and also reducing their value in relation to average earnings. Both of these measures make being out of work less attractive.

Trade union reform

Taking away legal power from trade unions makes it harder for them to push up wages through the threat of industrial action. It also makes it easier for firms to determine terms and conditions that are more favourable to the business when recruiting workers, which will encourage firms to hire workers.

Changes in legislation

Employment contracts often give workers favourable terms (e.g. the minimum period of notice given and the right to redundancy pay), which make it harder for firms to get rid of workers when they are not needed.

While good for workers, these increase costs for firms. Making it easier to hire and fire workers by reducing workers' rights laid down in their contracts makes it more likely that firms will employ people (as they know it is easier to shed labour if it is no longer required).

Making it easier to recruit and to lose workers will improve labour market flexibility.

8 Explain one drawback in cutting welfare benefits.

Answer on p. 120

Industrial supply-side policies

Making particular industries more responsive to market forces should increase both output and employment within that industry. This follows from the idea that industries with a monopolistic structure (or close to it) will have lower output levels and fewer people will be employed as a result. There is also the issue that industries operating in uncompetitive markets generally charge higher prices than those in competitive markets.

Supply-side policies here will focus on making a market more competitive. This will involve a number of approaches.

Deregulation

The term **deregulation** is usually used in the context of removing regulations that would previously have prevented competition. The removal of regulations should open up a market to allow multiple firms to operate. The removal of barriers to entry should lead to increases in output, less complacency by firms, lower prices and higher quality of output.

Privatisation

Private sector organisations are usually run for the benefit of the owners (shareholders in the case of companies). This 'profit motive' encourages the firms to strive to boost profits as the owners will benefit from increased rewards/returns. The profit motive should encourage firms to take decisions that improve efficiency, cut costs and increase production.

A public sector organisation does not keep any profits — these go back to the government as income. Therefore, it is believed that **privatisation** is a policy that encourages firms to become more efficient through the profit motive.

Examples of privatised businesses in the UK are British Gas and British Telecom — both of which became much more profitable in the private sector.

> **Deregulation**: the removal of regulations, usually to allow more competition into a market.
>
> **Privatisation**: the sale of a public sector organisation to the private sector — designed to improve the efficiency and profitability of the business.

Now test yourself

9 What might be undesirable about the policy of privatisation?

Answer on p. 120

Other supply-side policies

There are other ways to boost the supply side of an economy, as set out below.

Training

Encouraging firms to spend more on training should increase the capacity of an economy. This will be achieved in two ways:
- improved productivity
- reduced occupational and geographical immobility of workers

A supply-side policy would take steps to make training more desirable — this might be achieved through the government providing training schemes for the unemployed, or providing subsidises or tax incentives to firms that spend money on training.

Now test yourself

TESTED

10 If training is good for the economy, why does the government choose not to subsidise most, if not all, forms of training?

Answer on p. 120

Education

A highly educated workforce should increase the economy's capacity. Here, the supply-side policy would focus on ensuring education meets the needs of the economy. This is not easy, as attempts to introduce work-related qualifications into the school and college curriculum have not always been popular. It also requires planning ahead as it takes a number of years to introduce educational change, and the government needs to assess how the UK will develop in the future.

Apprenticeships for school leavers have received more attention in recent years: these should allow more workers to develop skills that would boost the capacity of the economy.

Infrastructure

Infrastructure refers to the physical capital that facilitates business activity and includes railways, roads, communication systems, etc. Governments can invest in these to make it easier for business to operate. For example, the proposed high-speed railways between London and Scotland will make it easier for business to be conducted throughout the UK. Similarly, expansion of London airports should make London and the UK more attractive to overseas businesses.

Entrepreneurship

Governments can make it easier for people to set up their own businesses. Either directly, or (more recently) indirectly, the government can offer assistance to entrepreneurs. Reduced 'red tape' in the sense of fewer administrative and legal burdens on small business will encourage people to set up their own enterprises.

The economic effects of supply-side policies

REVISED

We have stated that successful supply-side policies will shift the LRAS curve further to the right by increasing the capacity of the UK economy. There are other effects on macroeconomic indicators.

Effect on GDP

Increasing the capacity of the economy should lead to higher GDP. It should certainly increase the trend rate of growth in the economy. Of course, GDP requires both AS and AD, and so far we have only referred to AS. Therefore, for supply-side policies to boost GDP, they need to be used in conjunction with policies to manage aggregate demand.

Effect on unemployment

Successful supply-side policies should lead to lower unemployment in a number of ways:
- Lower income taxes will encourage people to take jobs as work becomes financially more worthwhile.
- Reduced welfare benefits will discourage people from remaining out of work.
- Deregulation of markets should increase competition and this should mean higher output and more jobs (though the increases in output may come from efficiency gains rather than employment gains).
- Improvements in education and training should lead to reduced occupational and possibly geographical immobility.
- Investment in infrastructure should attract more businesses and jobs to the UK, and should also reduce geographical immobility as people find it easier to work further from their home.

Effect on inflation

Successful supply-side policies should lead to lower inflation in a number of ways:
- A higher capacity for the economy means AD can be increased before capacity is reached. This means demand-pull pressures will not emerge until a higher level of real GDP is achieved.
- Trade union reform should ease cost-push pressure as there will be less upward pressure on wages by trade unions.
- More competition in certain industries will mean it is harder for firms to increase their prices due to declining monopolistic powers.

Effect on the balance of payments on current account

Supply-side measures should improve the balance on the current account:
- The downward pressure on prices outlined above should make UK exports more price competitive.
- A more productive workforce should also lead to lower-priced UK output.
- Quality of output should improve if investment takes place in education and training, and this should also lead to greater demand for UK exports.

Limitations of supply-side policies

REVISED

Supply-side policies have not always been popular with the country as a whole. This is probably because:
- Tax cuts often favour those with high incomes (e.g. cutting the 'top' rate in the UK from 50% to 45%).
- Cutting benefits is more likely to increase poverty.
- Reducing the rights of workers may prove unpopular with workers, who make up three-quarters of those of working age.
- These policies often take many years to show significant effects.

Revision activity

Make a list of the weaknesses of using each economic policy.

Summary

You should have an understanding of:
- What monetary policy is and how it affects the main economic indicators.
- How decisions on interest rates are decided upon.
- How changes in the exchange rate affect macroeconomic indicators.
- Fiscal policy.
- How fiscal policy affects the national debt.
- How changes in fiscal policy affect macroeconomic indicators.
- How the government uses a variety of different taxes.
- How the supply side of the economy affects the long-run growth rate.

- The distinctions between supply-side improvements and supply-side policies.
- How various supply-side policies work.
- How fiscal policy can also work as a supply-side policy.
- How changes in any of the above policies would affect the following macroeconomic variables and be able to show these policies through an appropriate AD/AS diagram:
  - GDP
  - unemployment
  - inflation
  - current account of the balance of payments

Exam practice

HS2 — the proposed high-speed rail link

One factor that determines the long-run growth of an economy is its infrastructure. More investment in infrastructure should improve the economy's potential growth rate. Therefore it would appear that the building of HS2, a high-speed rail link between London and Scotland (via Birmingham, Manchester, Sheffield and Leeds) is a good idea. However, opinion is divided.

The Chancellor, George Osborne, believes that it will create jobs outside London, which are needed given the fear that too much investment in the UK goes to London. It will also cut journey times significantly, in some cases slashing the journey time to London in half. Quicker journey times can also improve long-term growth and can encourage more businesses to locate in the UK due to improved travel time for workers. However, some argue it will result in more people working in London, so taking money away from other cities.

Critics say that HS2 is too costly, with the first estimate of its total costs of £33 billion now having to be revised to over £40 billion. The flipside of this is that it will provide an enormous boost to the economy, creating 22 000 jobs in building the line and 10 000 jobs in running the line once finished. Others claim this boost could have been injected elsewhere in the economy, for instance by upgrading existing railway lines or extending airport capacity.

1 Define the term 'long-run growth'. [3]
2 Explain two ways in which the building of HS2 might affect the current account of the balance of payments. [6]
3 Explain two ways in which the building of HS2 will generate higher economic growth in the UK. [8]
4 Analyse the negative consequences for UK economic performance of spending £40 billion on HS2. [10]

Answers and quick quizzes online

ONLINE

Now test yourself answers

Chapter 1

1 B All other answers are positive economic statements because they can be tested and subsequently declared to be true or false. Answer B is a normative statement since it is a subjective opinion, or value judgement: the word 'should' often suggests that a statement is an opinion.

2 C Oil in the North Sea is a naturally occurring resource, which economists classify as the factor of production known as land; A and D would be classed as capital equipment; B would be classed as labour.

3 Because the vast majority of resources are limited in supply, i.e. they are scarce. Individuals, firms and governments also have finite incomes.

4 In a free market economy, consumers will send signals via the strength of demand to firms in order to determine what will be produced. Firms will then aim to maximise profits and so attempt to produce goods and services in the most productively efficient way. Who gets the goods and services produced will be determined by consumers' ability to pay for them. In a centrally planned economy, all decisions will be made by the government.

5 D £8000. This question contains lots of extra information designed to test whether you understand the essence of the concept of opportunity cost. The only relevant information is that John can either keep or sell the car, missing out on £8000 if he chooses the former.

6 (a) Point Z is productively inefficient, since it is inside the economy's PPC. Output of one or both of consumer goods and capital goods could be produced with existing resources. There is a waste of scarce economic resources arising from unemployment of one or more factors of production.

   (b) Points A and B are both on the PPC and so are productively efficient. Maximum possible output combinations are being produced at any point on the PPC, including A and B. At either point, it is not possible to increase the output of one type of good without reducing output of another.

   (c) Point Y may be achieved in the future if the PPC shifts outwards sufficiently. This means economic growth is necessary, arising from an increase in quantity and/or improvement in productivity of one or more factors of production.

   (d) The opportunity cost, for example, of increasing the output of consumer goods by the amount RS is the loss of ML capital goods.

7 (a) An outward shift of the PPC due to more productive land.

   (b) An inward shift of the PPC due to a smaller population.

   (c) An outward shift of the PPC in the long run due to increased productivity of capital equipment in producing all goods and services.

   (d) An outward shift of the PPC in the long run due to more productive labour.

Chapter 2

1 (a) A leftward shift of the demand curve.

   (b) A rightward shift of the demand curve.

   (c) A leftward shift of the demand curve.

   (d) A rightward shift of the demand curve.

2 (a) 0.5 (inelastic)

   (b) 2.5 (elastic)

   (c) 3.3 (elastic)

3 Initial total revenue is 3000 × £1.50 = £4500. New total revenue is 3300 × £1.20 = £3960. PED is 0.5 (inelastic). Overall revenue has fallen by £540.

4 Total revenue will fall, depending on how price elastic holidays to the Maldives are.

5 Milk can be considered price inelastic.

6 (a) −3 (inferior)

   (b) 2.5 (normal/luxury)

   (c) 4 (normal/luxury)

7 (a) 0.75 (substitutes)

   (b) −0.8 (complements)

8 Excess supply.

9 Firms would have to reduce the price of the good in question in order to sell all their stocks. This would lead to both a contraction along the supply curve as firms have less of a profit incentive to produce the good, as well as an extension along the demand curve as more of a good is demanded at a lower price. Eventually the forces of supply and demand achieve a state of balance and a new, lower equilibrium price is reached which 'clears' the market of any excess supply.

10 (a) The demand curve shifts to the right, leading to an increase in price and quantity.

   (b) The supply curve shifts to the right, leading to a fall in price and an increase in quantity.

   (c) It depends: if cars become more popular, the demand curve for petrol will shift to the right, leading to a rise in price and quantity. However, if there is an overall reduced need for petrol, the opposite will happen.

   (d) The supply curve shifts to the right, leading to a fall in price and a rise in quantity.

11 (a) e.g. fish and chips

(b) e.g. lamb chops and wool

(c) e.g. land may be used for building houses or shopping centres

(d) e.g. the demand for pilots is derived from the demand for long-distance travel for holidays and business trips

12 D

Chapter 3

1 Production refers to total output, whereas productivity refers to the rate at which output is produced.

2 450/3 = 150 cups of coffee per employee per day

3 D

4 C

5 C

6

Quantity of footballs sold	Total revenue (£)	Total fixed costs (£)	Total variable costs (£)	Total costs (£)	Profit (£)
10	50	100	20	120	–70
20	100	100	40	140	–40
30	150	100	60	160	–10
40	200	100	80	180	20

Chapter 4

1	C	4	B
2	C	5	D
3	B		

Chapter 5

1	C	6	D
2	C	7	A
3	C	8	B
4	D	9	C
5	B	10	D

Chapter 6

1 2.25%

2 It has risen but at a slower rate.

3 UK = $46 015; Norway = $96 153

4 Possible answers would include:
- It is a sign that the population is enjoying a higher standard of living.
- Taxation revenue will increase, enabling tax cuts elsewhere.
- More government can be financed through higher taxation revenue.
- Any budget deficit can be reduced through reductions in welfare expenditure.

5 They are still rising but at a slower rate (3% down to 2% rate of increase).

6 Possible reasons:
- People may not qualify for benefits if they are still looking for work.
- People may not wish to claim for benefits for personal reasons.

7 Possible reasons:
- Motivation at work may fall (due to low pay, poor conditions).
- Inappropriate training provided to workforce.
- Teething problems exist with new technology.
- Rapid turnover of employment (people moving between jobs, etc.).

8 Index numbers are useful when it is the change in a price that matters more than the actual price of a good. Index numbers make it easier to see the magnitude of changes in the variable and can also be used to contrast with other variables that have also been translated into an index number.

9 Possible reasons:
- Inflation does not account for quality improvements.
- Trends in what we actually buy may change before the basket used is updated.
- Personal spending habits may differ significantly from what is in the weighted basket.

10 (a) Those items are more significant in terms of how the typical household spends its money.

(b) Trends in spending habits change — as incomes rise over time, the proportion spent on essentials should decline, which means the weights used need to alter. Additionally, as new products emerge, people may switch to buying these.

Chapter 7

1 Total expenditure and total income should be the same as they are looking at the same set of transactions but from different points of view. When we spend our money we are generating incomes for the supplier of whatever we are spending our money on. If we stopped spending, this would lead to falls in income elsewhere.

2 (a) €840 billion

(b) 5%

3 Possible problems with real national income are:
- It does not take into account the distribution of income.
- It does not take into account welfare provision for the poorer members of society (which determines their standard of living).
- How government spending is distributed will affect living standards (e.g. spending large amounts on national defence doesn't directly contribute to most people's living standards).
- Living standards will depend on the provision of public and merit goods.
- Non-financial factors will matter, such as freedom of speech, democratic rights, and so on.
- Environmental degradation may be serious and will not show up in national income statistics.

4 It is not in equilibrium. Total injections add up to £800 billion whereas total withdrawals add up to

£765 billion. As it stands, national income will change to bring the economy back into equilibrium.

5 (a) rightward shift in AD

(b) leftward shift in AD

(c) leftward shift in AD

(d) rightward shift in AD

6 Although extra spending will generate income and this in turn leads to more spending, this process is finite. Any extra income received will not all be spent. Initially the extra income will be taxed. Out of this now smaller amount of extra (disposable) income, some may be saved. Even if it is spent, some of this extra spending may leave the domestic circular flow because it is spent on imports. Therefore, with each extra 'round' of the multiplier process, a smaller amount is passed on. This means the rises in income quickly fall to small amounts after an initial boost.

7 (a), (b) and (c) rightward shift in SRAS

(d) leftward shift in SRAS

8 Reduced subsidies will make childcare more expensive. This will make working (and using childcare) less attractive, especially among new parents, so reducing the number of people willing to participate in the labour market. This reduced labour supply means less can be produced at full capacity (hence the leftward shift in the LRAS).

9 (a) D

(b) C

(c) B

10 An AD/AS diagram should show both a rightward shift in AD and a rightward shift in LRAS leading to a new equilibrium position with higher real GDP — which should lead to lower unemployment.

Unemployment will fall due to the expansion of AD — the extra spending by the government on education will have a multiplier effect on the economy and lead to a greater increase in spending, meaning there is a greater demand for output and more workers are required.

Unemployment may also fall due to an expansion of the productive capacity of the economy (rightward shift in the LRAS). This is because the investment in education should reduce occupational immobility of labour and increase its productivity (though these effects may take time to work).

Chapter 8

1 C and E

2 The rise in investment will lead to a rightward shift in the LRAS as well as a rightward shift in AD. The government will encourage investment because:

– Higher investment raises the productive capacity of the economy (increased LRAS), which means the economy can be expanded with less risk of inflationary pressure.

– More investment will boost AD and have multiplier effects on the economy (leading to reduced unemployment and higher GDP).

– Higher investment may also boost efficiency, which potentially will lead to more exports.

3 It is most likely to achieve:

– minimised unemployment

– economic growth

– reduced budget deficit

It is unlikely to achieve:

– stable inflation

– balance on the current account of the balance of payments

4 There would be a leftward shift in the AD curve caused by a negative wealth effect. This is likely to have negative multiplier effects in the economy. As households feel less wealthy, they will cut back on consumption and will borrow less to finance credit-related consumption. This means there is likely to be a rise in unemployment due to the reduced AD. The government's budget is likely to move closer to, or further into, deficit.

5 (a) structural — occupational immobility

(b) cyclical

(c) structural — geographical immobility

(d) frictional

6 When there is a positive output gap, actual growth is higher than trend growth. This means spending (AD) is above its long-term rate of growth. In this case there will be increased demand for output, and so for more workers. Hence, unemployment will fall.

7 Deflation refers to a fall in the average level of prices. Low inflation refers to a period in which prices are rising but at a low rate.

8 A leftward shift in AD can lead to deflation. This is due to lower demand leading to lower real output; there will be less demand-pull pressure on prices and firms may cut prices in order to sell surplus stock.

A rightward shift in SRAS can lead to deflation. A fall in the cost of production (e.g. falling material costs) will mean firms are willing to supply more at any price level and this will lead to a surplus of output, so firms will cut prices in order to clear this.

9 (a) improve

(b) improve

(c) worsen

(d) worsen

(e) worsen

(f) improve

10 A negative output gap involves growth that is below average and, as a result, unemployment is likely to rise. This may be associated with a reduced current account deficit, an increased budget deficit and falling inflation.

A positive output gap involves above-average growth and, as a result, there is likely to be inflationary pressure. Unemployment should be falling and the budget deficit will also be falling. However, the current account deficit will widen as imports rise with spending.

11 If inflation is demand-pull in cause, then attempts to reduce it will involve reductions in the level of aggregate demand. This will take spending out of the economy. Lower spending will mean less demand for output and therefore fewer workers will be required and (cyclical) unemployment will rise. Hence, there will be a conflict.

Chapter 9

1 Any of the following:
   - higher consumption due to lower monthly mortgage repayments
   - higher consumption as credit-financed consumption is cheaper
   - higher consumption due to saving being less rewarding
   - higher investment as the cost of borrowing to invest is reduced
   - potentially a boost to exports as lower interest rates are likely to lead to a lower value of sterling

2 The MPC will look at a variety of factors. Reasons for a decrease in the bank rate despite rising inflation include:
   - The rise in inflation is due to one-off cost-push pressure (such as a rise in indirect taxes) and is not expected to lead to ongoing rises in inflation.
   - The inflation rate is still below target and therefore lower interest rates are still needed to boost AD (and raise inflation back to target).
   - The rise in inflation is not expected to last and the forecast over the next 2 years is for downward pressure on inflation — remember that changes in interest rates can take up to 2 years fully to work.

3 If the debt is expressed as a percentage of national income, then rising prices (i.e. inflation) will reduce the value of this debt. Debt is expressed in nominal terms, whereas national income is expressed in real terms. This means that the significance of the debt will diminish over time due to rising inflation.

   Another possibility is that as long as the budget deficit is smaller than the growth in national income, the addition to the national debt will be smaller than the growth in national economy — i.e. both will grow in size but the denominator (the national debt) will grow faster, shrinking the ratio.

4 (a) (i) £880; (ii) £3880; (iii) £7403
   (b) (i) 5.9%, (ii) 12.9%, (iii) 16.5%
   (c) The system is progressive as the average amount of tax paid rises as the income of the individual rises.

5 A regressive tax is one where people on lower incomes pay a higher proportion of their income in that tax. If VAT is placed on essential goods then it cannot be avoided, and because VAT is a flat rate of tax (usually 20%), it will account for a higher proportion of a poorer person's income.

   Some would disagree, though, arguing that essential goods are usually subject to zero VAT. As a result, poorer households are unaffected. For example, food, prescription charges and children's clothing are zero-rated; electricity and gas bills have a lower rate of VAT (5%) attached to them.

6 The cut in income tax should lead to higher consumption, thus shifting the AD curve to the right. It should, according to supply-side theory, lead to a rightward shift in the LRAS curve as more people will be willing either to work longer hours or to take jobs as a result, thus increasing the productive potential of the economy.

7 Most full-time employees cannot choose how many hours they work. Choosing to work additional hours is more likely to occur in a manual job or in a part-time job. Therefore cuts in income tax make little difference to the majority of workers in full-time, non-manual employment.

   In addition, cuts in income tax may simply make people 'better off' so they do not need to work longer hours (this is known as the 'income effect').

8 It may lead to poverty among those affected — making it harder for them to get back into the labour market.

9 There are a number of problems that might arise:
   - The sale of shares in the privatised company may not be successful — normally, though, the shares are priced at a level that encourages investors to buy.
   - Regulation may be required if limited competition emerges in the industry.
   - People may be excluded from consuming a good that is socially desirable (e.g. people might be unable to access heating and lighting in adequate amounts).
   - Prices of the good may rise, which is unfair on poorer households.
   - Job losses may occur in that business as it aims to cut costs and improve efficiency.
   - Output may not be as high as expected; for example, rail and bus services may be cut if they are deemed unprofitable.

10 Reasons include:
   - Subsidies cost money which carries an opportunity cost — money could have been spent elsewhere.
   - Not all training will be effective in raising productivity or reducing labour immobility.
   - Firms are the major beneficiaries of a trained workforce — they should be encouraged to pay for it.
   - All the costs are short term but the benefits may only be gained in the long term.
   - Would the government know what training is 'best'?
   - Administration costs in setting up and implementing the scheme.